The Pursuit of Your Creative Call

This book is dedicated to the late
Paul Gordon
*Who played a major role in me accepting
the Lord Jesus Christ in my life.
I am forever grateful
Rest In Peace.*

In Loving Memory Of A Dear Friend
Pastor Noah Barefoot, Jr.

The Pursuit of Your Creative Call

Mel Holder

ARMOUR OF LIGHT
PUBLISHING
Chapel Hill, North Carolina • Charleston, South Carolina

Copyright © 2011 by Mel Holder

Without limiting the rights under copyright reserved above, no part of this publication may be reproduced, stored in or introduced into a retrieval system, or transmitted, in any form or by any means *(electronic, mechanical, photocopying, recording or otherwise)* without the prior written permission of the author and owner of this book. The scanning, uploading and distribution of this book via the Internet or via any other means without the permission of the author is illegal and punishable by law.

Please purchase only authorized electronic editions and do not participate in, or encourage electronic piracy of copyrighted materials. Your support of the author's rights is appreciated.

Published in the United States of America by
Armour of Light Publishing
P.O. Box 778
Chapel Hill, North Carolina 27514

www.armouroflight.org
www.thepursuitofyourcreativecall.com

Design by Michael E. Evans

Cover & Interior Art by Oswald Green and Kelsey Kalem

ISBN 978-0-9825476-7-0

Library of Congress Control Number: 2011941779

First Edition

All scriptures quoted from the Authorized King James Version unless otherwise noted.

10 9 8 7 6 5 4 3 2 *1*

ENDORSEMENTS

"Mel Holder has always been one of my favorite Gospel Jazz artists, I am so excited about his new book which is a further extension of his creative genius."

Eric J. Chambers,
Jazzspel Host/Executive Producer
The Word Network

"Matt 22:14 says, 'For many are called, but few are chosen.' If you know you're called, this is the book for you, to unlock the unsearchable riches that God has given you! Few people will choose to be all that God has called them to be. But with Mel's insight and testimonies of overcoming obstacles, you will be encouraged, to believe God, that you have what it takes. Your gift will make room for you! By the end of the book, each reader will possess the courage, to be a part of an elite, set apart group! Few are chosen - Are you one of them? Read, The Pursuit of Your Creative Call and you will be!"

Pastor Tyronne Stowe
Gospel 4 Life Church • Chandler, AZ
Former NFL Linebacker

"Mel has been a blessing to the body of Christ for so many years with his music in worship and praise. We've been looking to bring him to Nigeria for some time. With his new book, The Pursuit of your Creative Call, I believe it is now imperative for us to bring him. You will be greatly blessed by this book."

Pastor Seye Kosoko
RCCG Mercyplace
Lagos, Nigeria

"Brother Mel, shares magnificent keys that will inspire and ignite your passion. It will also encourage you to discover God's calling in your life from dream to reality. I DARE you to pickup this book, I'm sure you will enjoy the journey. It will be one of the most pleasurable experiences that you've ever had before."

Pastor Jay Amina Sr.
Oahu, Hawaii

"In this new age we need a call from the Divine, I pray that this book may be useful to the world and that it would be a blessing to the nations and it strikes everyone's heart. Those who read this book will surely hear the 'Creative Call'."

Pastor M.B. Jeevan
Visakhapatnam District, India

If by chance you have ever thought about giving up on a dream, a vision or a desire, you will have a clearer understanding of your path after reading "The Pursuit of Your Creative Call". Mel opens up your heart and mind to discover who you were created to be in your Kingdom walk. If you need direction with your God given assignment, this is a must read.

Minister Earl Bynum
Executive Minister of Music
The Mount - VA/NC
Syndicated Radio Show Host
Rejoice Musical Soulfood
International Gospel Recording Artist

"Thank God for the gift He has given Mel Holder, for it has brought about a great change in our world. For the changes we make today, cause our tomorrows to be different from our yesterdays."

Bless you Mel
Your Friend,
Pastor Kenneth Joyner

Working with Mel Holder as my music producer has proven to be a creative feast. After reading this book I have a deeper appreciation for his creativity.

Gerald Alston
Gospel and R&B singer
With "The MANHATTANS"

"I read The Pursuit of Your Creative Call in one day. The Lord's presence was real and I felt as if HE was speaking to me. I began laughing, crying, praying, re-affirming my call and decreeing life over my talents. Mel Holder brings a new depth of revelation to your Creative Call. His insights bring clarity to the purposes of God for the individual and the church at large. He has identified the barriers that block one's path to reaching all that God has and unlocking the talents inside.

Mel is an authentic, prolific teacher, motivational speaker, an anointed genius who God has raised in this Kairos season to communicate in such a practical yet relevant, with unique humor regarding ones journey to their creative call. I highly recommend this book to all my friends, churches, and ministry groups! This is a manual that should be used across all ministry departments. When you pick it up, it will be hard to put down! It is personal, biblical, informed, compassionate, analytical and encouraging! In the midst of these pages the reader will understand the significance and importance of their creativity and why there is such a heavy price tag on their calling."

Dr. Sheryl Reaves
Fresh Fire Intercession Ministries
Santa Clarita, CA

"In a time and in a place where mediocrity seems to be the mantra of the day, it is exciting to the Body of Christ to embrace Mel Holder's new book, 'The Pursuit of Your Creative Call', which encourages God Class-Excellence in all that we do for Christ."

Dr. Deborah A. Godwin-Starks
CEO Quasi Inc, Stellar Women on the Move
WQSW 100.5 FM, college professor, and author

ACKNOWLEDGMENTS

First I want to thank God for giving me the gift of life, and now, through His Son Jesus Christ, I have the Gift of Eternal Life. As a result of this gift, I am able to experience and enjoy many earthly relationships. At the top of the list are my parents, Sinclair and Doris Holder, who gave me the physical gift of life and who dedicated their lives so my life can be what it is today. Dad, I know you are a witness to this from your heavenly home. Mom I thank you for your continued personal sacrifices.

To Brittain and Nicky, I thank you for your understanding, dedication and relentless support. You have extended yourselves way beyond the call of duty. I Love You All So Much!!

To my Pastors, Dr. A.R. and Elder Karen Bernard, thank you for consistently challenging me to expand and grow in every aspect of my life.

To all my spiritual fathers and mentors, Bishop Courtney McBath, Dr. Jerry Grillo, Bishop Otis Locket, Bishop Paul Thomas, Pastor James Corbett and Bishop Roy E. Brown, I thank you all for your spiritual guidance and leadership, this book would not have been possible without what God allowed you all to pour into my life.

Lloyd Evans, this book is a result of your investment in me twenty years ago. Again, I say thanks.

Henry Davis, your dedication and loyalty to me over the past ten years is truly appreciated. God has clearly placed you as an anchor in my life and ministry.

Rev. Mal Williams thanks for your friendship and tenacious efforts in opening so many doors.

Dino and Cheryl Kartsonakis, thanks for presenting the platform for me to share my musical gifts on your Television Show.

Cheryl Williams thanks for your obedience to God who has allowed you to support and work with my ministry.

I want to thank Michael E. Evans, Myron "Dub" Putnam, Ruben Holder, BJ Cephas, Oswald Green, and Kelsey Kalem for your countless hours of dedication in seeing this project through.

To my family at Trackworkz, Tony Prendatt, John Kiehl, Craig Davis, Rob Cavicchio, Mike Panteleoni, Thanks for embracing my talents and allowing me to take this creative journey with you.

To my creative team, Thurston O'Neal, Latasha Jordan, Larry & Marissa Felder, Loris Holland, Jimmy Miller, Gerald Alston, David Russell, Sam Hendricks, Travis Milner, John Smith, John Palmer, Lanee Battle, Johnny Mercer, Jerry Elock, Phil & Brenda Nicholas, and Randy Gilmore. Thanks for your musical collaborations throughout the years.

To my support crew in Jamaica, West Indies, Pastor Greg Morris, Arnold Kelly, Nadine Bair, Norma Minto, Sandra Harris, Paulette & Fernando Morgan, and Lavene Elloit White, Thank you.

To The Christian Cultural Center Band and Performing Arts Ministry, Thanks for allowing me the occasion to grow and develop while serving with you.

To my colleagues in ministry, Rev. Robert Lowe, Rev. Kenny Hammond, Rev. Nathan Best, Pastor Tyrone and Lady Stowe, Pastor Jay Amina, Pastor Edwin Bullen, Pastor Magapu Jeevan, Pastor Gary Lee, Rev. Johnny Coleman, Rev. Mary Tumpkins, Rev. Sheila McKeithen, Rev. Cleveland Hoby, Rev. Eric Chambers, Bishop Joseph Alexander, Rev Gordon Williams and Pastor Winston Pierre, Thank you for the support and fellowship. I never would have made it this far without you all.

Additional thanks to:

Andre L. Carter, Brian Osborne, Gerald Peoples, Alberto Reyes, Dr. Sheryl Reaves, Elder Lavern Tillery, Keith Childress, Cheryl Hope, Steve & Rose Gable, Rebirth Christian Bookstore, Jamie Forte, Victor Bolton, Marlon Charles, Clive Scott, Lawrence Lewis, Adrian Cox, Kenny Denard, Bishop Anthony Slater, Tammy Greene, Rawlins Joseph, Pastor Steve Belgrove, Maurice Powell, Rev. Paul Tribus, David Fritz, Gary George, Herb Spencer, Ian Holmes, Adrian Nurse, Mario Murray, Cynthia Bell, John Wilson, Roger Samuels, Pastor Anthony Gilmore, Adrian Aguard, Rev. Holgate, Madeline Alexander, Marlene Mason, Charles Maynard, Shannon Rice, David Robinson, Carl Peels, Mama Curtis, Mary Tilman, Diane Jones, Dawn Brady, Pastor Edward Davis, Pastor Jerome Myree, Hubert Eaves, Rob Robinson, Bishop C.R. & Sister Ann Parker, Brawn Hampton, Michael Faust, Bishop Charles Blake, Pastor Kim Brown, Randy Legoin, David Wallcot, Jay & Patricia Hewlin and Steve Reid.

And deep appreciation to:

Mike Woods, President & CEO, Black Network TV
The Honorable Mayor Stephen Tripp, Ayden, NC
Chief Jones, Ayden Volunteer Fire Department

Mel Holder • 3 Years Old

*"Train up a child in the way he should go:
and when he is old, he will not depart from it."*

Proverbs 22:6

TABLE OF CONTENTS

Endorsements	5
Acknowledgments	9
Introduction	17
1. First Things First	21
2. The Process	25
3. Ready	31
4. Set	39
5. Go	45
6. What's Talent?	51
7. Making It Happen	57
8. Amazing Abilities	63
9. Called	69
10. Focus	75
11. Purpose	81
12. Finding Your Lane	87

13. Positioning	93
14. Prep Work	99
15. Hindrances	107
16. Choices	115
17. Faithfulness	121
18. Corporate Service	129
19. Law and Order	137
20. Show Me The Money	143
21. Relationships	153
22. Options	159
23. Maximizing	165
24. Ministry	173
25. Fellowship	183
26. Seed	189
27. Maturity	197
28. Battles	205
29. Moderation	211
30. Usage	217
31. Priorities	225
32. Environment	233
33. Conspiracy Theory	239

34. Provision for Vision	247
35. Right Mind Set	255
36. Difficult Situations	261
37. Frustration	267
38. Who Are You Really	275
39. Service	283
40. Practical Application	289
41. My Pledge	297
About Mel Holder	301
The Music of Mel Holder	304

ERASMUS HALL INSTITUTE OF PERFORMING ARTS JAZZ BAND

"Praise ye the LORD. Praise God in his sanctuary: praise him in the firmament of his power. Praise him for his mighty acts: praise him according to his excellent greatness. Praise him with the sound of the trumpet: praise him with the psaltery and harp. Praise him with the timbrel and dance: praise him with stringed instruments and organs. Praise him upon the loud cymbals: praise him upon the high sounding cymbals. Let every thing that hath breath praise the LORD. Praise ye the LORD."

Psalm 150

JUNIOR HIGH **BIBLE SCHOOL**

INTRODUCTION

Every great hit song began with an idea. One word can spark a thousand speeches and one idea can revolutionize the world. One plan can defeat the most gigantic giant and one vision can cause a people to rise up from the ashes of bondage to the opportunities of freedom. One mustard seed can birth a forest and one talent can be transformed into the next superstar.

Inside of each one of us is a fire that is unquenchable. This fire is the very essence of God Himself in man. It is with faith that we are able to release this fire. You see without faith it is impossible to please God. Once faith is activated it leads to an irrefutable path to success. This is seen across the world where there are people just like you and me who feel the fire and are constantly finding themselves in the factory of faith where dreams are manufactured and, where millions of voices are proclaiming the new thing that God is birthing in and through them. The miracle of God inside of you creates an undeniable need to share this creative call.

The awesome expression of your creative call is ever increasing, and yet you wonder how you will know which door to open, which opportunity to accept and which direction to take. Shakespeare said "All the world's a stage and all the men and women merely players. They have their exits and their entrances, and one man in his time plays many parts."

The thrill that happens when your talent is awakened from its slumber, the emotional roller coaster ride you feel will never end as you begin to learn that there is more and more and even more to discover of this treasure inside, this fascinating fire that forges future fame and fortune.

And in the middle of all of it lies a deep and resonating bell, the clarion call that asks a million questions that are left unanswered. Why am I here? What is my purpose? In the deepest valleys of sleep you will find that dreams supernaturally announce their arrival with such intensity that upon awakening there is a hint of urgency still left in the corners of your mind. And as you tend to the daily tasks, these nocturnal revelations arrest you on the subway, in the car, at the gym, in the studio, on the set and even at church.

Here it is again, this force that hits your spirit, soul and mind with such speed you can hardly catch your breath. While there is no picture to look at, you can see this epic adventure playing on the screen inside your mind. It is so vivid, so persuasive, and so powerful that it actually defies description and your natural comprehension.

It encompasses you like a whirlwind. It shakes you from the bottom of your feet to the top of your head as one explosion after the other shakes you into action. The passion to produce this purpose looms like a tsunami rising up inside you, surpassing your ability to articulate it, or even worse, it is so bold, so daring and so new it outpaces traditions and even your fears. In the pursuit of this newborn desire you will find others like yourself, those not satisfied with the ordinary and content with the status quo. You will find yourself moving intensely towards things that may even seem unconventional, irrational, incredible and exciting.

This conflict ultimately propels you toward the very reason you were created. Finally, you are now engaged in the pursuit of purpose and destiny. You are about to find out who you are, and why God impregnated you with such a jewel known as talent. Long before you even knew yourself God prepared a personal blueprint with your name on it. The orchestration of the melody of your life was written ages before the inception of Adam and Eve. God authored something in you that He did not share with even the angels. He gave you and me the power to create.

This book is a map that will guide you to the place where you can use the keys to the kingdom and unlock your destiny once and for all. God has provided the keys. All you have to do is put the key in the lock and turn it. For some, unlocking the door and walking through it is a simple task. For those who cannot find the courage to use the keys, they often find themselves wandering through life in timeless uncertainty.

You will have to make an effort to discover your life's calling. The first step to finding the answer is to find the one with the answer, God. Connecting with God will result in you connecting with your calling. All it takes is a little effort, time, patience, and personal perseverance. If you can relate to any part of this, then you are in pursuit of 'the call.' Of course it helps to have the key and a bit of guidance along the way, and that is why I am confident that this book will serve as a GPS and assist you on this journey.

If you feel that strong urge towards a career, a vocation, a profession or occupation, then you are ready to discover a wonderful life. Allow me to invite you to join a very elite crowd of people who fought all odds to find their way to their calling. When they did, they changed the world around them, and many continue to do so today, even in their time of sunset. They still impact the world because they found the key. Who knows?

Maybe you are the next Michelangelo, Mahalia Jackson, Martin Luther King, Jr. or even Michael Jackson! I believe you can be!

There is a blessing for you in the midst of these words which will be revealed as you read this book. It has taken my entire voyage to date to learn these truths and I share them with you from a servant's heart filled with love and appreciation to God for His kindness to me. If any of you are like me, I am sure at one time or another you have pondered these thoughts and questions "Why has God entrusted me with something so precious?" "Why can't I get it out?" "Why can't I make it plain?" "Why can't it go away?" Better yet, "Why can't I just let it go? "WHY LORD?" Why have you placed me on this path which is "THE PURSUIT OF YOUR CREATIVE CALL?"

Creatively Living In Him,
Mel Holder

CHAPTER ONE
~FIRST THINGS FIRST~

I am truly honored and elated that you are taking the time to read this book. It is my desire that some word or thought will galvanize you and have a positive impact spiritually, intellectually, creatively and naturally on your life. If you are reading this book, then it is safe to say you have established your relationship in Christ and are looking for growth and development.

Congratulations! That being established, you are free to skip to Chapter Two. On the other hand, if you are reading this book and have not already established your spiritual journey by asking Jesus Christ to become your personal Lord and Savior, then let me be the first to invite you to answer the first call from God on your life.

Having Christ in your life would give you the key to unlock any uncertainty of your purpose and calling, naturally or spiritually.

Christ came to redeem us back to God the Father by pardoning our sins. That is our first and primary calling, to have a relationship with Christ and our Heavenly Father. So, if you have not accepted Christ, let's stop right now and give you an opportunity of a life changing experience, which will usher you into the most exciting season of your life! It all starts by recognizing that you are a sinner and are in need of the redemptive process, which can only be accessed through Jesus Christ. Are you ready for a life change? If so, simply say this prayer and passionately believe it!

Father God, I understand that sin is a transgression of your law. I acknowledge that I have sinned against your laws, which have put me in a broken relationship with you.

I am deeply sorrowful for my transgressions, and I want to turn away from my past sinful life right now and come before you asking your forgiveness.

Lord God, please forgive me of my sins and cleanse me from all unrighteousness and help me not to fall into sin again.

I believe that your son, Jesus Christ, died for my sins, was resurrected from the dead, is alive and hears my prayer.

I invite Jesus to become the Lord of my life, to rule and reign in my heart from this day forward.

*Please send Your Holy Spirit to help me obey you
and to do your will for the rest of my life.*

In Jesus' name I pray, Amen.

If you prayed this prayer for the first time today I want to welcome you to the family of God and your new life in Christ. Now that you have started on this new journey there are a few steps you need to follow. I want to encourage you to grow closer to Him, and the Bible tells exactly how to follow up on our commitment. From personal experience, let me suggest these few steps that I believe will help you in your new walk with Christ.

~ First ~
Find a Bible-believing local church where you can fellowship, worship and grow spiritually.

~ Second ~
Tell someone about your new experience in Christ.

~ Third ~
Spend time daily in prayer and reading God's Word.

~ Fourth ~
Get baptized in water as it is a commandment of Christ.

Fast Forward:
†
Did you pray either one of these prayers? If so, are you now ready to experience the greatest adventure of your life?
†
Are you committed to a local fellowship and are you ready to offer your talents for God's glory?

NOTES

CHAPTER TWO
~THE PROCESS~

For those who are reading this book who have started the process and have established your relationship with Christ, this is a perfect time to renew your vows and commitment to Him, so join me as together we whole-heartedly repeat the following:

Father God, I humbly come before you asking for your forgiveness of any sin of commission or omission. Jesus, I thank you for being my personal Lord and Savior. I once again ask you to renew my relationship with you and restore me once again to the place where you are my first love. Holy Spirit, please baptize me once again and refresh my soul, heart and mind. In Jesus' name I pray, Amen.

After you have prayed this prayer there are a few fundamental steps you should follow:

~Step One~
Increase your time in worship.
Worship is the key to God's heart.

~ Step Two ~
Increase your time in prayer.
Prayer is the key to intimacy with God.

~ Step Three ~
Increase your devotion time in the Word of God.
God's word is the power of salvation.

~ Step Four ~
Encourage someone else in God.
Receiving is giving.

~ Step Five ~
Renew your commitment to service.

The past ten years have been a very exciting period in my walk with Christ, not to mention my musical development and public ministry. In this vital period is where I grasped the understanding of the call of God on my life. I can look back on the years prior to my commitment to God and see how He was leading me even when God was nowhere on my radar. God had me in his thoughts and was guiding me to my purpose.

At the age of nine I curiously picked up a clarinet that my older sister had brought home from PS 189, the public school we both attended in the Brownsville section of

Brooklyn, New York. When I actually think about it, her bringing home the clarinet was not an accident at all. God chose to use her to introduce to me His purpose and plan for my life. God's purpose always has a challenge hidden deep in side of it and this one was no different.

What made this challenge so interesting was that I had asthma! Playing a woodwind instrument requires a great deal of lungpower and there were times when I had little to none. So breathing normally was a challenge to say the least, much less having the wind to play the clarinet. God used the obedience of my sister to present to me a situation that would open the door to my destiny. The minute my lips touched the reed on that clarinet and I heard the sounds pouring out, and I was hooked.

And what was even more exciting was that I realized I had musical abilities. I forgot I had asthma. I refused to let it keep me from the joy I felt when I was playing the clarinet. Day in and day out my love for music grew until I suddenly realized playing music was the only thing I wanted to do.

Following the discovery that I had a passion for music, I remember listening to 'Kool and The Gang' and imagining myself being a part of the band. I would stand in front of the mirror and imitate what I had observed while looking at pictures on their album covers. Don't laugh. All around the world there are young people looking in their mirrors while dancing, acting or playing air instruments. And by the way, there are some who are holding a Bible in their hands preaching to invisible thousands as the Holy Spirit prepares them for their role in reaching the lost. What we all have in common is the revelation and realization that God has placed something deep inside of us that demands we give it life.

Throughout my early years I began to familiarize myself with the bands and groups of that era. Such groups as the legendary Earth Wind and Fire, Mandrill, Crown Heights Affair, Chicago, Ohio Players, BT Express, just to name a few. I also remember every Friday when my mother would allow me to stay up late so I could watch Don Kirshner's Rock Concert. The show aired from 1973 until 1981. It was syndicated and produced by Don Kirshner himself and featured live performances which were a rarity at the time. Many of the other shows featured lip-synched performances to pre-recorded music tracks. It didn't matter to me. I loved every minute of it. Another one of my favorites was the famous "Midnight Special" it was a weekly musical television series that aired during the 1970s and early 1980s, created and produced by Burt Sugarmann for NBC.

These shows featured all the top groups of that period. I did not realize that what I was doing was schooling myself for the future. I learned what not to do on stage as well as what was considered appropriate. On one hand I was watching and listening to music that excited me, thrilled me and inspired me. On the other hand I began to apply what I had seen and heard to the talent burning deep inside me.

Some people may not think those programs have any bearing on someone's calling, but let me assure you that in my case they did. My gift was maturing through my passion for music that God placed in me. This passion drove me to hear and experience other musical talent which influenced my own learning and development. When you realize that GOD is the source of your talent you will long to perform for Him. It is that passion to serve Him that makes the journey so exciting.

Imagine your talent as a car. We all know it takes gas in the tank before the car goes anywhere. Our passion is much like the gasoline, which drives the car. Without it we go nowhere.

If a car cannot move without gasoline, why would we expect our calling to develop without passion? Passion is that compelling emotion which motivates and drives one's ambition. The most exciting thing about passion is that you can create it, nurture it and increase it. All it takes is devotion and commitment. Got it? Great! Now that you know what your car looks like and the gasoline necessary for it to run, let's talk a bit more about the vehicle God has given you, your calling!

God does not need Allstate, Geico or Progressive, He never has an accident.

Fast Forward:
†
What challenge do you face in order to accomplish what God has placed in your heart?

Can you honestly say that you have the passion that is necessary to arrive at your point of destiny?

NOTES

CHAPTER THREE
~READY~

*"Relationship is a key component to the worship experience…
And is more important than performance!"*

Now that we have established the fact that the call of God on your life is the vehicle which God has assigned to you to drive, it is time to take delivery and responsibility for this vehicle. In order for God to fully trust you with the keys to the car, He first will expect you to spend a definite time of instructional driving with someone who has mastered driving a destiny vehicle.

Imagine you are driving on an obstacle course where you are certain to come across a myriad of uncertain twists and turns.

You are a bit nervous due to the fact that this is a new road you are on and the road signs are all new to you. The first thing you do is to buckle up so you will not be injured in case you are faced with potential danger. Just like in the natural world where a seat belt protects you from serious injury, your spirit man needs the Holy Spirit to be fully operational in order to provide protection. I think we all would agree it is critical to be strapped in while traveling on rough and painful roads. What we all too often forget is that the road we travel is never smooth. I am reminded of the road Christ had to travel in his last hours on this earth. The Via De La Rosa, the street where Christ walked on his way to Calvary, was not smooth by any stretch of the imagination. As the street wound through Jerusalem it became more and more rugged.

At Golgotha the Jesus ascent became rough and rocky. Jesus had already been beaten by a cat-o'-nine-tails until his back was ripped apart. He had a crown of thorns crushed into His skull and had to carry his own cross until he physically could not continue. Once the cross was on the shoulders of Simon of Cyrene, Jesus was able to stumble his way to his death. It is recorded that not one time during his horrible torture did he ever utter a word.

I am not sure I could do that; how about you? He was able to endure this terrible ordeal because of the glory that was to come. He knew that once he had accomplished this task that every man, woman, boy and girl would have access to God once again. Salvation was just up the road on a hill called Mount Calvary.

When you look at the road you are on with all its twists and turns, potholes and cracks, do you ever wonder how in the world you will ever arrive at your destination of Destiny? Jesus had to deal with both mental and physical issues.

In like manner, you and I have to overcome our mental response that says the pain is too intense and the price is too great. So, what is it that gives us the ability to go through whatever it is we face in order to achieve our goal? I personally have found that standing on the Word of God is the key to me being able to stand up to anything and everything that comes my way. Stand on God's word and believe his promises.

CLAIMING THE PROMISES OF GOD
"He [Abraham] *staggered not at the promise of God through unbelief; but was strong in faith, giving glory to God"*
Romans 4:20

When I was growing up I loved physical challenges. Some of them required almost nothing to accomplish while others seemed almost impossible. I can still hear my personal trainer yelling in my ear "no pain no gain!" To be completely honest, overcoming the obstacle requires a discipline and principle that extends far beyond mere physical training. Of course it is painful to deny yourself of physical pleasures. It also takes a great deal to overcome your mental and physical desire to give up.

What I want you to grasp in all this is the fact that to overcome your fleshly desires requires that you die to yourself. Your personal wants, desires, passions and plans must be laid on the altar of sacrifice before God, willingly. Once you lay your life down for the sake of the call of God on your life, God will lift it up again so that He might be glorified. Is there pain in dying to your own desires? Of course! It might be more mental or it might be more physical, but dying to 'self' so Christ may live will produce pain.

You must make the choice which kind of pain you are willing to face, either the pain of making your mind up to obey Godly discipline or the pain of regret when you realize you want your desires more than all the wonderful rewards God has for you. One of the more wonderful secrets God has unveiled to us is that He is always ready to hear our prayer! Calling on God anytime is a good time.

CALLING ON THE LORD FOR HELP
*"Help us, O God of our salvation,
for the glory of thy name: and deliver us,
and purge away our sins, for thy name's sake."*
Psalm 79:9

The pain of Godly discipline means you are willing to make a present day sacrifice to endure whatever you must so that you can be assured of His blessing in your life. Preferring your worldly desires might bring about momentary rewards, but it offers no lasting anticipation of future blessing. It's a terrible thing to realize that you were robbed of your future all because you didn't want to discipline yourself.

Too many people rob themselves of their future because they want to live in the moment. There were times that I fell victim to this. I would take short cuts and allow myself to do things that were dishonest. This type of behavior is common in the music industry. Having said all that, let me share with you a completely different order and way of doing things that apply when you are operating in God's purpose. When we operate in our calling we should always try to do our best. However the focus should never be on how well we perform, even though excellence in performance definitely has its place. The main objective is simple. We are to give God all the glory in all that we do.

First of all, your immediate attention and desire must be focused on God while you acknowledge His greatness, glory and deity. Your spirit man connects with the Holy Spirit and your natural man begins to decrease. That is how you will know the spiritual discipline is happening. As we enter into the realm of praise we give God honor in our thoughts and words.

"All the nations you have made will come and worship before you, Lord; they will bring glory to your name"
Psalm 86:9

It's from the depth of our very being where we connect with God the Father, The Most High. What really happens is what begins as a creative performance becomes a worship and praise offering which ministers to God. The key difference between creative performing and ministering is who is getting the glory. When we minister to the Lord it is not about us, who we are or what we do. It's solely about God, Christ and the Holy Spirit; the Three in One.

Secondly, when we enter this form of ministry we are engaging in personal or individual worship. This is fine; however, that is only one vital stage. True worship includes many characteristics that are in constant operation in your life, you should be drawing from them constantly on a daily basis. True worship occurs when we acknowledge Him as Master and humble ourselves in submission to the

Lordship of Jesus Christ by professing His position in our lives. I want to share the following components of what I have come to know as essential to our preparation to serve the King of Glory, as artists and believers.

FELLOWSHIP

When Moses had face-to-face fellowship with God, he was glorifying God and the glory of God was literally shining upon him. What an awesome experience to have! Here was Moses, face to face with God in His presence and God's glory was still visible on his face for hours afterward. I want you to grasp the power of this situation and realize that it's impossible to be in the presence of God and not be affected.

"And it came to pass, when Moses came down from Mount Sinai with the two tables of testimony in Moses' hand, when he came down from the mount, that Moses wist not that the skin of his face shone while he talked with him"
Exodus 34:29

LORDSHIP
Making Christ Lord is foundational
to our relationship with Him.

"And that every tongue should confess that Jesus Christ is Lord, to the glory of God the Father"
Philippians 2:11

RIGHTEOUSNESS
A life that operates in godly righteousness gives God the
power to work through that life.

"Being filled with the fruits of righteousness, which are by Jesus Christ, unto the glory and praise of God."
Philippians 1:11

FAITHFULNESS
"And they overcame him by the blood of the Lamb and by the word of their testimony; and they loved not their lives unto the death"

Revelation 12:11
*Our obedience brings us closer to God.
Our faithfulness reveals our true character.*

Fast Forward:
†
What challenge do you face in order to accomplish what God has placed in your heart?
†
Can you honestly say that you have the passion that is necessary to arrive at your point of destiny?

NOTES

CHAPTER FOUR
~SET~

*Fellowship among the brethren is essential for our growth…
And it brings God glory.*

Next, we arrive at the moment called 'SET.' This is the stage that many would like to bypass because this place can be painful in that it involves pruning many things out of our lives. When you arrive at this stage you will be required to give attention to time, effort and endurance as it relates to your talent, praise and worship and service.

Jesus, in his earthly ministry, spent a great deal of time at the place called 'SET.' This first occurred when Jesus went up to the mountains. Jesus was not caught up in ministering to the multitudes at this point. He knew that He could only be effective if He got away from the masses for a while so he could hear clearly from His heavenly Father and understand the future steps of His calling.

You will never be able to reach the full manifestation of your call until you have spent ample time with God.

If Jesus, being the Son of God and having the highest fellowship with God, needed this time then, there is no question we need to spend time with God in order to find out the direction for our lives. The daily lifestyle and ministry of Jesus was a constant sacrifice of praise and thanksgiving to His Father in Heaven. We must learn to do the same and not just on Sunday at church.

PRAISE

Jesus exemplified an attitude of gratitude and it produced in him, and his followers, a heart of thanks giving.

"Whoso offereth praise glorifieth me: and to him that ordereth his conversation aright will I show the salvation of God"
Psalm 50:23

"I will praise thee, O Lord my God, with all my heart: and I will glorify thy name for evermore"
Psalm 86:12

THANKSGIVING

"For all things are for your sakes, that the abundant grace might through the thanksgiving of many redound to the glory of God"
2 Corinthians 4:15

"And one of them, when he saw that he was healed, turned back, and with a loud voice glorified God"
Luke 17:15

It is extremely important for us to remember that God's power can heal not only our sicknesses, but the sicknesses of others. Our compassion for those in physical need should be a distinctive component of our service to Christ. Our knowledge of His healing power should resonate in every aspect of our ministry. We often experience suffering as a believer. However, it is only for a season. God will allow us to suffer through things that He knows we can endure. When we have learned the core value of any season of suffering He will allow us to understand the reasoning behind it all.

HEALING
"When Jesus heard that, he said, This sickness is not unto death, but for the glory of God, that the Son of God might be glorified thereby."
John 11:4

As a musician I understand the importance of being in the place called 'SET' from a secular perspective. You cannot do an excellent performance without proper preparation. It is the hours which are spent rehearsing that ultimately give you the power to perform at the highest levels.

"Public performance is an extension of private practice."

There is no difference to this principle when it comes to the preparation needed on the spiritual side. In fact, it may even be greater. When you are 'SET' you are ready and equipped for service. Your gifting operates with a new dimension of authority and effectiveness as you spend time with God perfecting those gifts He has bestowed in you. Once we have come to realize our worship creates an environment and atmosphere where God can inhabit; He will show up and bless and anoint the gifts we have offered to Him as a sacrifice of praise. When our hearts are pure and our motives are to prepare a sanctuary for Him we will then witness His glory in our midst.

"So that the priests could not stand to minister
By reason of the cloud: for the glory of the LORD
Had filled the house of God."
2 Chronicles 5:14

Stepping into the glory of God while using your gifts has a phenomenal response attached to it. You will suddenly, without actually realizing it, operate in your calling on a totally higher level. Things that were stumbling blocks before are now seen as stepping stones. When you are 'SET' you are operating under God's anointing. This anointing will give you the ability to lead the nations to Christ and to train them in worshiping Him.

"All nations whom thou hast made shall come and worship
before thee, O Lord; and shall glorify thy name."
Psalm 86:9

Fast Forward:
†
What challenge do you face in order to accomplish what God has placed in your heart?
†
Can you honestly say that you have the passion that is necessary to arrive at your point of destiny?

NOTES

NOTES

CHAPTER FIVE
~GO~

When it's time to 'GO' God will always start you off with something or some place that you may view as substandard. My first encounter with what I thought was a substandard position was when I was required to clean the bathrooms for the ministry where I got saved. When I first began I was having a hard time with the task at hand, but as time went on I began to understand there was absolutely nothing wrong with cleaning the bathroom in the house of God.

HUMILITY
When we think more of God and less highly of ourselves, our life will reflect that choice.

*"But God forbid that I should glory,
save in the cross of our Lord Jesus Christ,
by whom the world is crucified unto me,
and I unto the world."*
Galatians 6:14

The challenge for me came from the fact that I had already achieved a certain status and position in the music industry and felt that this bathroom cleaning task was a bit beneath my station in life. I learned that my pride had to be dealt with in order for God to truly use me for His glory. While I may have felt I was suffering in my flesh, it was nothing compared to what Christ was willing to do to ensure my salvation. The experience of cleaning the bathroom was something I would learn to deeply appreciate as time went on.

SUFFERING
"Yet if any man suffer as a Christian, let him not be ashamed; but let him glorify God on this behalf."
1 Peter 4:16

You may have dreamed of walking out on some huge platform before thousands of people applauding in anticipation of witnessing your performance. There is nothing wrong with dreaming that way, but realize this very important fact, that our dreams are not always in God's plan. When God presents you with one of those insignificant opportunities according to you, remember that the outcome lies in your response. The truth is that our flesh will rarely react positively to humble beginnings.

The sooner we learn that God is presenting us with circumstances to test and train our servant's heart the faster we will arrive at our destiny. We may not see this as an act of love, but it is. God never disciplines anyone He does not love. We must understand that the God of the universe is taking time to perfect our relationship with Him. That in and of itself is an awesome realization!

When you love someone, you like to tell them how much you love them. The best part of telling someone this is their response in telling you they love you too. Love is given and love is received. One of the most wonderful truths I have learned is that God loves me unconditionally. Even when I fail, fall and stumble, He still loves me. When I am going through a trying time He is always there to comfort me.

DISCIPLINE

"For ye are bought with a price: therefore glorify God in your body, and in your spirit, which are God's."
1 Corinthians 6:20

"I beseech you therefore, brethren, by the mercies of God, that ye present your bodies a living sacrifice, holy, acceptable unto God, which is your reasonable service. And be not conformed to this world: but be ye transformed by the renewing of your mind, that ye may prove what is that good, and acceptable, and perfect, will of God."
Romans 12:1-2

GIVING

"Whiles by the experiment of this ministration they glorify God for your professed subjection unto the gospel of Christ, and for your liberal distribution unto them, and unto all men."
2 Corinthians 9:13

BEARING FRUIT
*"Herein is my Father glorified, that ye bear much fruit;
so shall ye be my disciples."*
John 15:8

The first evidence of bearing fruit is seen when we begin sharing our faith with others and winning others to Christ.

"And many of them that sleep in the dust of the earth shall awake, some to everlasting life, and some to shame and everlasting contempt. And they that be wise shall shine as the brightness of the firmament; and they that turn many to righteousness as the stars for ever and ever."
Daniel 12:2-3

A GOOD WORKS WITNESS
"Let your light so shine before men, that they may see your good works, and glorify your Father which is in heaven."
Matthew 5:16

"Having your conversation honest among the Gentiles: that, whereas they speak against you as evildoers, they may by your good works, which they shall behold, glorify God in the day of visitation"
1 Peter 2:12

We can produce the fruit of the Spirit by adhering to the Word of God.

"But the fruit of the Spirit is love, joy, peace, longsuffering, gentleness, goodness, faith, meekness, temperance: against such there is no law."
Galatians 5:22-23

Ultimately it is our belief in Jesus Christ that gives us the power to do all things.

BELIEVING IN JESUS CHRIST
*"Jesus saith unto her [Martha],
Said I not unto thee, that, if thou wouldest believe,
thou shouldest see the glory of God?"*
John 11:40

It became real to me that when God allowed me to experience those trying situations it was not so that He could see if I loved Him. He knew I loved Him. What we go through is there to reveal the part of us that is faithful and the part of us that is unfaithful. In the end, the decision to choose either path is left up to us.

The real test is whether or not we are going to complain about singing and sharing words of encouragement to those who are at the hospital sick and shut in. Are we going to withhold our best just because we are asked to teach a group of younger children? If you are faithful over the smallest of things God will know, as well as you will know, that you are worthy enough for Him to bless you with greater opportunities.

Fast Forward:
†
What are you doing right now that you know God has you doing but you are not happy doing it?
†
List three things that are being developed in your character as a result of obedience to humble beginnings.

NOTES

CHAPTER SIX
~WHAT'S TALENT~

"Your talent can be a vehicle for entertainment, but has more value when it is motivating and inspiring."

Your talent is an instinctive, personal endowment usually inborn and granted exclusively by God. The uniqueness of talent is what makes an individual special in our society. While we all have the same capabilities to experience life there are those among us who have a somewhat heightened capability, capacity, competence, endowment or intelligence in certain areas. We generally look at talent as it is recognized in the entertainment arena, but there are other skills that should also be seen in this light. Some individuals may express this ability in areas such as philosophy, theology, finance, education or politics while others express it through tailoring, carpentry, plumbing, painting and the list goes on and on.

The world celebrates those who have extraordinary talent, especially those who entertain us. Whether it be a Michael Jackson in the music and entertainment arena, or a Michael Jordan in sports or a Barak Obama in politics and government, the world celebrates their accomplishments. All the seminars and self-help books in the world can't put most people in the same league with a Jackson, Jordan or Obama.

These extremely talented individuals bring joy, inspiration and hope to our lives and society at large. There would be little purpose in the gifting of these talented individuals if their gifts were not meant to be shared with the world. Should Michael Jackson, Michael Jordan and Barak Obama isolate their talents and keep only to themselves, that isolation would be an enormous waste and a great disservice to mankind. These men not only excelled in their talents but gave their talents to the world for inspiration, encouragement and entertainment.

"Your potential is a picture of what you can be, your faith allows you to see the picture and accomplish it."

The reality is that most of us do not possess the talent of a Jackson, Jordan or Obama. That is not to say we are worthless. Quite the contrary! God has given each one of us a precise talent and ability to complete our personally designated assignment. God did not make a mistake and short change you. He carefully distributed to you the talent that was necessary for you to be complete. Without any question, He has prescribed for you the correct dosage of whatever is needed to be all that He intended you to be. This concept is chronicled in the parable of the talents.

The parable of the talents, or pounds, is all about a master who is going on a trip. Before he leaves he entrusts his property to his servants. His property was worth eight talents which was the value of all he possessed. One servant was given five talents, the second servant was given two and the third servant was awarded one. The master came home and asked his servants to give an accounting of what they did with the property he had entrusted into their hands. The first two servants had put their money to work and doubled it. The third servant had hidden his money in a hole in the ground. He was punished for his laziness! The master was delighted with the servants who did something with their talents.

*"There is great joy and fulfillment
when you are able to have your talents
working in the purpose and plan of God for your life."*

If we are to please God we must increase whatever He gives us. In doing so, we honor Him. Sad to say there are still some of us who are like the servant who hid his money in the hole. There are three very distinct reasons why you may find yourself in this position.

1. Un-confessed Sin:
Sin is a transgression of God's law and any transgression brings forth a break in our fellowship. When we are in broken fellowship we forfeit the benefits of God's presence. It is essential that God's presence is in our life to operate in His plan and purpose.

2. Lack of Discipline:
Discipline is the bridge between our thoughts and actions. We can mentally desire to have God's

purpose and plan in operation in our lives, but until we do something about it this will never happen. God never forces His will on us. He gives us the opportunities to make choices and decisions.

3. Confidence:

You may encounter a moment in time when you may lose confidence in your talent. Those are natural feelings by virtue of your humanity. We must come boldly to the throne of grace where we will find mercy and grace to help in the time of need.

Even when we have little or no confidence God requires us to take action. In the act of obedience we will receive the necessary tools to obtain God's purpose in our life. We are deceived in our thinking once we begin to believe that we have nothing to work with. You are not talent poor!

Throughout history there have been many who have achieved prominence in their field and have done so by vigorously and vigilantly exploring their natural talents. It is this characteristic that distinguishes them from others. Using their talent is easy because they are using those abilities that are most natural to them. Their accomplishments, by and large, appear from their appreciation of those talents in themselves, and their comprehension and understanding of how to use them as often and as effectively as possible.

When it comes to spiritual service, the best place to be is where you are forced to trust God and not rely on your talent. Once you are secure in your relationship with God and the talents He has given to you then you should begin to make substantial progress. What are you currently doing with your talent? Are you allowing fear to convince you to do nothing? Are you complaining about all the things you don't have and never stop to realize that God has given you a customized personal blue print which includes every possible ingredient for your success?

Maybe it's time you realize the wonder and splendor of what God has entrusted to you. You have been given a talent that will glorify God if you choose to allow it do so. The choice is yours.

"When your belief is concentrated and you exercise your faith, it unleashes the power of God...and all the supernatural resources imaginable."

Fast Forward:

What are you doing to invest and grow your talent?

What dividend have you received from talent investment?

NOTES

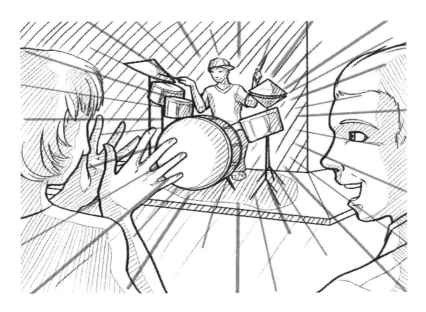

CHAPTER SEVEN
~MAKING IT HAPPEN~

I have never seen a book titled
"Be Michael Jordan in Thirty Days."

Every year there are thousands of books published on the topic of self-help and developing personal skill sets covering a wide category of subjects. There are books on how to increase your parenting skills, how to increase your computer skills and even on how to become a good Christian. I have yet to see a book published on how to get talent. The reason why is because you cannot teach talent. It is prearranged without any kind of democratic process. You either have it from birth or you don't. You can earnestly pray for God to increase your skills and ability, but your talent is already predetermined by God and is locked into your DNA.

In the arena of professional sports, a talent evaluator always covets talent first, even if it's raw and undeveloped. If all you have are skills, your talent cannot be developed; conversely if you have talent, skills can be developed. Talent is truly an innate ability that can be improved, but only to a certain level. In contrast, a skill is defined as a developed and learned or acquired ability. A person with little natural talent always has the ability to improve. His devoted efforts will ultimately hit a point of diminishing returns when his performance is compared to others with more natural talent.

"God is the only one who can birth talent."

Training, practice and experience will improve your skills and take them a great distance. But they can never produce talent. Creative artists in ministry should have the desire to use their talent in order to experience the depth in ministry that produces current, future and eternal success. We can witness the fruit of this success through our obedience to God. In our obedience we can use our talents as a tool which can positively transform lives through the power of God. While this all sounds wonderful, there is still a very deep and profound question we must ask ourselves. What is required to reach this goal? We can search the scriptures and find many possible answers, but I would like to point out two things that might help to answer the question.

First, you should follow your heart. I am not talking about your fleshly heart that has a personal agenda. I am referring to that still small voice within the fabric of your being that you have come to know as the voice of God. Now let me explain that statement. That still small voice is like an echo from heaven that you sense deep in your spirit. It is so powerful and full of purpose that most people would swear they heard an actual voice speaking; it is that strong.

When I think about this, I really get excited and I hope you do too. Here we have the Creator speaking and creating a heart that responds to His very Word. It is this issue of the heart that makes it so important for us to read the Word of God and meditate on it day and night. King David had some insight into matters of the heart when he said, *"I have hid Your Word in my heart, Oh Lord, so I might not sin against You!"*

There is power in the Word of God, and its power is unleashed in unfathomable dimensions when it resides in our heart. It speaks to every situation we face by using a still small voice. When we are in His presence and in His Word, we find insights that make it easier to use our talents and gifts for Him. When we look closely at what it is God has for us to do, we will always discover that it is bigger than we could ever imagine. How exciting to realize that we are living our lives in response to the still small voice of God deep inside.

Secondly, you should live your life to its utmost potential. It's not enough just to do what matters to you. You should also "up your game" to the fullest so that not only you benefit but others can benefit as well. Personally I feel the deepest level of satisfaction occurs when I know that I've used my talent and given my all to God and in return someone else has been blessed by that effort. Honoring God with our talent means just that, giving our very best in service to Him and His people.

Your growth as an artist is determined by your willingness to use your skills, talents and abilities so that you can add greater value to yourself and the Kingdom of God. Here are a few tips I believe will assist you in making improvements.

1. Develop your learning skills.
Never stop obtaining knowledge on any level. What you don't know will often hurt you, and in some cases it could kill you. There is an old axiom that states "God does not hold us accountable for what we don't know, but He does hold us accountable for what we do know!" Never allow ignorance to carve out a place in your life. Using your talent is wholly based on the ability to comprehend and learn new things.

2. Your surroundings are very important.
Surround yourself with people who are on the same journey and are seeking similar success. Having these vital relationships will help to keep you motivated. Motivation is an essential ingredient to learning skills. If you are excited and passionately interested in a particular subject matter, you will be motivated to learn and absorb new information.

3. Be flexible.
Never be so set in your ways that you cannot be open to new and different ways of doing things. Being flexible essentially means you are sensitive to the Holy Spirit and know how to quickly come under authority and be subject to those in leadership. When you operate with a flexible mind set, you anticipate that change is a part of personal growth.

Fast Forward:

†

How are you currently using your talent?

†

What obstacles are in the way of you using your talent in ministry?

NOTES

CHAPTER EIGHT
~AMAZING ABILITIES~

How you recognize amazing ability is when something extraordinary occurs around an ordinary moment.

From "AMAZING GRACE" to amazing abilities, the maturation process of the church has now displayed a wealth of talent second to none. Our houses of worship have in my opinion the best talent on the planet. This is nothing new to the church, from as early as the 1930's and 1940's many talent scouts have gone to church to seek out their next star. Many of our top artists started right in the church.

When I begin to think about amazing abilities, I am reminded of the accomplishments man has made in the past one hundred or so years. Man has gone from walking to racing in the most sophisticated automobiles ever created. We also went from flying kites to flying spaceship missions to the moon. Our homes no longer have an ice box but a refrigerator and freezer. Instead of a small black and white television we now have sixty inch flat screens less than two inches thick. In the music industry we have gone from wind up turntables to Ipods.

Not much has remained the same on any level due to the amazing abilities of people who make the most of a simple idea. What makes the difference is the amazing ability of each individual who can see, think or create outside of the box. When it comes to the kingdom of God, we also see great accomplishments. We continue to see the growth and development of churches. These churches feature an incredible vault of talent. It was at one of these churches that I found the building blocks for my own talent. I began my journey to learning how to become a musician who was dedicated to God.

My first public appearance was at the Junior Workshop at Bedford Central Presbyterian Church in Brooklyn N.Y. at the age of nine. There was nothing all that amazing about my musical ability at that time, but that appearance was the start of my creative call. Through all of the experiences I have had since those early days, I have learned that everything starts in a seed form and grows into a full blown experience.

At the age of nine I was working with nothing but raw talent until I made my decision to develop what God had entrusted to me. I realized that talent alone was not going to produce amazing ability. The people around me at that time made sure I realized there was more to developing my gift than just talent. I had to be willing to put in the time and effort to develop my talent, and the only way I was going to obtain success was through hard work. If you learn nothing else from this book, grasp this truth and hide it deep in your heart. Success is a natural result of work. Success never precedes work. As a matter of fact, the only place success precedes work is in the dictionary.

To arrive at the point where we can safely say we have come to some level of success, creative artists must exhibit an exemplary work ethic. We should also have a relentless drive to be a good witness in every aspect of our artistry. Our talents as well as our character and integrity should be an excellent representation of God to both the church and the world. There is no better witness for God than operating in excellence. On the other hand if we fail to accomplish excellence in our witness for Christ as well as our talent being dedicated to Him, people will see us in our imperfection long before they see the God in us.

It often baffles me to think that we could entertain even the idea of representing the author and finisher of our faith with substandard efforts. Unfortunately there are times we do exactly that when we do not walk in creative integrity. We should have a hunger to consistently build on our talent and should never become so comfortable in what we are doing that we develop a lackadaisical attitude.

We need to have and maintain a positive attitude towards learning. As we develop our learning skills, we will find that it's the smallest details that make the biggest difference. The difference between a very good singer and an experienced singer is the ability to execute the nuances of their vocal talent. For example, both the good singer and the experienced singer can sing 'Amazing Grace' at a high level of proficiency.

However, the differences come into play in the details of the performance. The more experienced singer will exercise her ear more efficiently and in return be more accurate with diction, pitch, tones and phrasing. It is all these elements that make up the total of one's talent. They may seem small but they make a huge difference in the performance.

Not too long ago while at a ministry event I heard a singer do a rendition of "Mary Had A Little Lamb." This rendition was absolutely amazing. What made it so good was the masterful interpretation. Even with this simplistic elementary melody the anointing filled the room. I then realized that when God gives the gift of great talent, He anoints it to become something truly amazing.

It's much like having the icing placed on an already delicious cake. What I want you to capture here is that this person was performing a children's song! It was not a classical piece of music by Mozart or a jazz standard by John Coltrane. The singer was clearly anointed.

> *"When you experience a master authority in any creative field, you will also sense their anointing on their talent and gift."*

The anointing is the tangible evidence that the Holy Spirit is in operation. There is no doubt that the anointing is the key unction which creates amazing ability. No matter what talent you might have or how hard you work at becoming a great artist, make certain that in everything you do the anointing is present. Begin with looking deep inside and take an inventory of your motives and especially your attitude.

Make certain your lifestyle brings glory to God and not concern from man. I pray you will look deep into your heart and search out the excellent spirit God has placed inside you so that you can empower your talents and gifts with the unction of the Holy Spirit's anointing. I have good news for you, when the anointing is present you will always produce amazing abilities.

Fast Forward:

†

What can you do to take your talent from the ordinary to the extraordinary?

†

What do you have to change in your life to better present your talents and gift?

NOTES

CHAPTER NINE
~CALLED~

*"Sometimes things are delayed…
But that does not mean they are denied"*

    First and foremost, there is something deep down inside that feels like a volcano about to erupt when you realize you are called to serve God. While the feeling is invisible and is hard to define, there is no doubting that it desires to be released. The first inclination of this call will be coupled with an intense desire to accomplish something that has a sense of purpose. As stated in Chapter Two, it will be coupled with a passion which is the gasoline to fuel the call of God on your life. When you are called by God, you will have a growing compulsion to use your talent for Him.

The second factor is that there is an external certification to your call. God uses mature individuals in ministry to reveal the calling on your life and often does so by introducing you to what is called the process of ordination. As a member of the body of Christ first, your local church body should recognize your gifts. The acknowledgment of these gifts and one's use for service in the local body varies vastly depending on the requirements set in place by those local assemblies. We have to be so careful not to confuse our calling with our career as our calling is much deeper. Our career is something that we chose. Many of us have been through several career changes in our life. Our calling is something that we either accept or reject, according to where our relationship with Christ stands at the moment the call is confirmed in our spirit.

> *"Our calling is something that is distinct and burnt into our total existence and purpose here on earth."*

Third, you must possess the ability to stay on course when you are challenged. After you have gone through stages one and two, you will encounter some level of resistance. In many circumstances this will come directly from individuals within the body who may even be close to you such as friends or family. Remember, at this stage of your spiritual development, Satan does not care that you are saved.

What poses a threat to him is when you get busy in the work of the Lord. Satan will try intensely to disrupt your progress at this stage. For me, it happened at a transitional stage in my spiritual development when I joined CHRISTIAN LIFE CENTER in Brooklyn, New York, a vibrant, rapidly growing ministry. I was very excited and felt strongly that this was the place where God was leading me. At that point in my Christian walk, I was certain and clear of the call that God had placed on my life. I inquired about the process to join the music department and become a musician on staff. I was told that I had to be a church member for one year and there were several required classes I had to take. I was somewhat disappointed to hear this as I knew I was called in the area of music ministry.

I also knew I was talented and felt I could contribute to the creative arts ministry right then and there. My vehicle was filled with the gasoline of passion and was raring to go. However, what I did not understand was the reasoning behind this process. At that point I had a choice to make. I could stick it out and go through the prescribed process or I could leave and go somewhere else where the requirements were not so stringent. God used this situation for me to see myself and develop my character.

*"I believe that every situation we encounter is…
Either God sent or God used."*

Many times we put more importance on our reputation rather than the development of our character. Satan was also there appealing to my humanity and ego. He knew that the success and the fulfillment of my destiny could be severed if he could circumvent me from going through the necessary process. I made a definite decision to go through the entire process and wait a year to join the music department.

To my surprise that year just flew by. I saw that the process had helped me to grow and it took my life to the next level. On the exact day of my one-year anniversary I inquired about joining the music department again and was told that there were no openings at that time but someone would be in touch with me soon. I waited another three months and still no one had contacted me. I began to grow furious. But God was not finished with preparing me yet. I had to remain patient.

The calling of God does not always seem logical or make common sense. A sense of compulsion will prompt the believer to understand that God may be calling him to the ministry. When God equips you with the gifts necessary for ministry these are sign posts that will let you know He has placed a call on your life. That sense of urgent commission is one of the central marks of an authentic call.

Second, there is the external call. Some believe that God uses the congregation to call out those who are called to ministry. The congregation must then evaluate and affirm the calling and gifts of the believer who feels called to the ministry. As a family of faith, the congregation should recognize and celebrate the gifts of ministry given to a certain member and take responsibility to encourage those whom God has called and respond with joy and submission.

The biblical challenge to "consider your call" should be extended from the call of salvation to the call to the ministry. John Newton, famous for writing "Amazing Grace," once remarked, "None but He who made the world can make a Minister of the Gospel." Only God can call a true minister, and only He can grant the minister the gifts necessary for service. The great promise of Scripture is that God does call ministers and presents these servants as gifts to the Church. Consider your calling.

Do you sense that God is calling you to ministry, whether as a pastor or another servant of the Church? Do you burn with a desire to proclaim the Word, share the Gospel, and care for God's flock? Has this call been confirmed and encouraged by those Christians who know you best?

When all these defining elements have been addressed and the gasoline tank of passion is on full, then it is time for you to set out on your journey. That journey will take you through many processes that will produce the necessary elements for service to God. There are no short cuts. There is no way around the process. Without it you will certainly fail. With it you will certainly succeed.

God still calls . . . has He called you?

Fast Forward:
†
Can you pinpoint the moment when
the fire of God entered your spirit?
†
Have you continued to nurture the flame, or have you allowed the distractions of this world to snuff it out?

NOTES

CHAPTER TEN
~FOCUS~

"Process is important, but you also gain power from results which come from narrowly focusing on the outcome."
Tom Peters – The Pursuit of WOW!

Focus is an incredibly important key to having a creative journey. The ability to focus can often produce a wealth of power and results. Without focus you may see movement but actually have very little progress. With focus you gain direction and purpose. When you are operating with clear direction and purpose you are able to produce tremendous things. Focus is much like water in a balloon. When you squeeze the balloon the water comes out with tremendous force. It is this focused force, which propels the contents into action.

Focus is not a spiritual gift we receive from God and it hardly ever comes naturally. Focus must be developed with definite and intentional steps. All too often we are faced with so many options, which actually become distractions. These distractions pull us in a myriad of directions, all prohibiting our ability to focus. What is even more disconcerting is that we often find ourselves spending much of our time and energy on things that really don't matter. For example, we may find ourselves so caught up in what someone feels about our talent, to the point where we become insecure. Once we fall prey to this we are headed in the wrong direction and in turn lose focus. Paul the apostle expressed it this way;

"Brethren, I count not myself to have apprehended: but this one thing I do, forgetting those things which are behind, and reaching forth unto those things which are before, I press toward the mark for the prize of the high calling of God in Christ Jesus."
Philippians 3:13,14

The obvious solution to this predicament is to focus on the things that are most important to our development, both spiritually and naturally. One of the ways to accomplish this is to set goals and target dates. One of the laws of success is to place concentration and all our energies in one central location. This requires looking neither left nor right but looking up to our heavenly Father for guidance and direction.

"Place your mind and focus on Him… He will direct and order your steps!"

If you truly desire to obtain a greater level of accomplishment with your talent, you will have to apply yourself and focus. Focus requires taking steps that are sometimes difficult. Many of us get lost the moment we take the first step. The reason this happens is because we have not established what our target is going to be. Just wanting to be a singer, musician, dancer, actress or athlete is not enough because those desires are too broad in and of themselves. You have to decide specifically what it is you want to do and break it down into the smallest of details.

When creating a detailed game plan for success, you must be careful not to become so distracted that you get little accomplished. Focus gives you the energy to create that much needed game plan.

I often think of the talented musicians who have physical disabilities. It would have been very easy for them to give up and place all their attention on their physical challenges. Stevie Wonder, for example, has been able to accomplish so much despite the peril of his disability. It is evident that his focus and persistence have propelled his God-given gift and talent. This enabled him to present to this world one priceless and timeless musical gift after another. There are people all over the world who face similar challenges but lack the mental discipline to stick to the plan to achieve success.

Something spectacular happens when we narrow our attention and focus on the goal we truly desire. The "WOW FACTOR" can only be discovered through this process. The mind does not reach out to attain any certain achievement until it has a clear focus on its objective. As artists, we dream of that moment when we are receiving a prestigious award such as a Grammy, Oscar, Emmy, Dove or a Stellar. Many of us may have gone beyond the point of just dreaming and have taken action to bring the dream into reality.

You may have applied yourself in your area of discipline and you may have made strides toward accomplishing the goal you set. Even with this effort you may not receive those lofty awards and accolades from your industry peers. But let me share something with you that I believe will give you hope. Focus always makes an impact! Just by striving to become better, you automatically increase your value. Even if you never win an award, you can shoot for the stars and be very effective. Focus will lift you to a new level if you will be dedicated, disciplined and determined. Focus can and will expand your vision.

Recently, while at one of the Grammy award events, I began to network with a few industry people. After numerous conversations with many of my colleagues, everyone agreed that receiving a Grammy required much more than just having a great recorded project.

This does not take away from the work and effort needed to produce a quality project; it simply reinforces the fact that there are many more ingredients that are needed to attain the prize. Many of these other ingredients may seem like trivial details. But when you are able to give attention to and focus on these elements, you will obtain the desired success. For example, once a recording project is completed, there is still a great deal of work beyond your talent needed to accomplish the kind of success that finds your name on a Grammy trophy.

Talent alone is not a recipe for success. Success usually finds those who have the most determination and focus!

We do not stay focused naturally. Just as light naturally loses its focus and gets diffused, so does a person's attention.

For that reason we should have accountability relationships-- people who will speak to us when we begin to lose focus. What I have learned about focus is that it is not an event, it is a process. Anytime you engage in a process, it takes time and effort. The result that comes from applying yourself can lead only to success. Success is the natural result of focused and structured steps that lead to the accomplishment of a predetermined goal.

It has been said; "If you fail to plan, you plan to fail." There is a great deal of truth in that statement. It is my sincere prayer that you will sit down and begin to make a plan that will lead you to maximize your talent and reach the success God intends for you to have. There may be times when friends or family will think that your plan is unachievable, but you must buffer those words with what God says. God tells you in His Word that *"all things are possible"* if you will just "believe" (Mark 9:23). He also tells us that we *"can do all things through Christ who strengthens [us]"* (Philippians 4:13).

You will never succeed on your own. It takes your working with God and others to achieve the focus necessary to achieve your goal and His plan for you.

Fast Forward:

†

Can you identify the things that hinder your focus?

†

On what goal are you currently focused?

NOTES

CHAPTER ELEVEN
~PURPOSE~

To fully understand purpose, we must first realize one very simple truth that God has a master plan prepared for us. All we must do is discover it. One of the first signs of discovery is when you begin to sense an inner certainty that you are called into ministry.

Your gifting will give a clear indication of how to understand where it is you fit in ministry. For example, dancers have the unique ability to move their limbs unlike anybody else. Singers have the unique ability to use their voice unlike anybody else. Musicians have the unique ability to play musical instruments unlike anybody else and all these talents serve as equipment for the sole purpose of fulfilling God's plan.

"What God has called you to do,
He gives you the equipment to get it done."

Your calling is a God idea. He is the one who has created you, and nobody knows what you are capable of doing better than Him. The plan for your life originated and was established by God with you in mind. He gave each one of us stewardship over our skills, talents and abilities in order for us to get a specific job done. God always has the significance of our calling in His mind. Our quest is to operate in total unison with that significance. In order for us to accomplish that task, we must have the mind of Christ. Once this is accomplished we will better understand our assignment.

Our assignment falls under the following headings:
A Reason!... A Season!... A Lifetime!

Everything God has called you to do that is related to your gifting has a purpose and a reason, even though in many circumstances we do not know it in its totality. This occurs because God's calling is a progressive revelation. That is why we have to exercise our faith and trust in God. God is actually protecting us from ourselves by giving us limited knowledge until the appropriate time when we are ready for more revelation. That is why we have to exercise our faith and totally trust God. Trust requires us to reason the purpose of our talents and gifts. The season of reason is the beginning of understanding. Reason always brings about the season of revelation that is so powerful it will last a lifetime.

In the beginning steps of our ministry, God will begin to reveal future steps and phases. It is very rare that progressive revelation is given in a complete form. It always unfolds as our gifts and talents are unveiled.

Most often God reveals just enough so that you have an overall understanding. God does not reveal to you the good or bad things which may occur during the process; neither does He tell you the price and sacrifices that are required. When you answer the call of God, it will move you into new areas you have never before ventured into. I must warn you that there is always a price to pay for any new found access. God's call defies human logic and comprehension. Things will begin to be revealed to us as we press forward, whole-heartedly trusting God.

> *"As you trust God, your vision will become…*
> *Clearer day by day. It is a process that will…*
> *Give you peace the more you rely on God."*

It was a few months after I had accepted Christ that I felt impressed to go down to Columbus Circle in Manhattan, New York and play hymns on my saxophone on the street. I really could not understand then why I was doing it, but even in my infancy in Christ I knew that He was leading me to do it. So, for days at a time, that is what I did, until finally one day I ran into some old classmates who were also musicians.

Much to my surprise these old friends began to talk about spiritual things. They were hungry and were in search of God but had no idea He was the one they were looking for. God had planned for that task to be accomplished through me. What an honor to share the love of God with my friends. A short time after this all took place I organized a Christian big band that we simply called "MUSICIANS IN CHRIST."

Shortly afterward I stopped playing on the street and realized the reason I had been doing it had been accomplished. There are some things that God places in our life that are there for the long haul and there are some things that are there for only a short time.

There are a few things though that we start with and should continue with all through our life. Prayer, our personal devotions and consecration to God are needed for the duration of our spiritual journey. Without proper preparation we will find ourselves missing one or more key elements that will ensure the success of our journey in discovering our purpose. When our will becomes subject to His will and we are not so headstrong that we demand things go the way we want them to go, then and only then will we release the plan of God so that it can manifest in the form of a revelation about our purpose.

I had to stand on the street and play hymns in order for me to learn how to discover just one small purpose, that being to lead my friends to the Lord and create a musical event that would be a witness for Christ. If I had been disobedient and not gone to the street to play, my friends might not have found Christ when they did, much less the wonderful joy of playing together. That one event gave me a season of revelation as I learned that when we offer God our dreams in exchange for His plan for us, we will then discover the reason and the purpose of our calling and gifts.

Fast Forward:
†
Can you clearly identify your purpose?
†
What is it that God has you doing currently in this season?

NOTES

NOTES

CHAPTER TWELVE
~FINDING YOUR LANE~

Imagine your purpose is given to you in the form of a car. You awaken one morning and walk into the kitchen. Oddly enough there are, lying on your kitchen table, a set of keys and a note that states your purpose is sitting in the driveway, ready to go. You hurriedly go outside and find the most awesome car you have ever seen sitting in your driveway. Even the license plate has your name on it, and the driver side door is wide open. You get in and begin to admire the interior and wonder if it really can go as fast as the speedometer reads. There is only one way to find out. Put the key in the ignition and turn it!

In order for this vehicle of purpose to go anywhere, it needs gasoline. The octane of the gasoline that powers our calling is passion. Without passion, our calling will go nowhere. On this journey we will encounter ups and downs, good times and bad times, not to mention places and faces we will pass along the way. We must have plenty of gasoline, or passion, and we must remember to drive in the right lane. To do otherwise could create problems for those who are on the road with us, not to mention our own personal harm. In my quest to find my lane, I had the opportunity to meet a very skillful and talented musician. It happened one Friday night at Rescue Church in Queens, New York.

A fellow saxophonist, Randy Gilmore, invited me to the service where Loris Holland was playing keyboards. Loris was older than me and immediately I looked up to him as my older brother, out of respect for his age and musical talent. They were both part of one of the more prolific Christian bands of that era, called "NEW CREATION." When I heard them play, I was blessed to hear Christian music performed on a high professional level.

At that time I also had a Christian band called "Musicians in Christ" (MIC), which was based in Brooklyn. On occasion we would perform at local events in the New York area. Every time I had the opportunity to share the stage with their group, I was truly blessed. A few years later I was searching to find a location to consistently hold my band rehearsal. I reached out to Loris and he was able to secure Pilgrim Church for me. After a few rehearsals, Pastor Roy E. Brown, Senior Pastor of Pilgrim Church, offered me the position of band leader. This gave me the opportunity to work closely with Loris who (I would come to discover) had perfect pitch!

I would constantly challenge him and test the accuracy of his gift. He had the ability to write intricate musical orchestrations in the oddest of places, like while sitting in the passenger seat of a car without using any keyboard.

Understanding that faith without works is dead, I not only prayed for this gift, I bought books on the subject and asked many questions and went to work trying to obtain it. What happened to me during this process is something I believe you will find very interesting. Over time, my pitch identification improved and I was able to write better musical orchestration. The more I worked at obtaining perfect pitch, the more frustrated I became. Believe me when I tell you working to obtain perfect pitch is difficult to say the least. I became so frustrated I got mad at God. I just figured He had short changed me somehow on the talent side. This battle went on for years.

One day it finally clicked in my spirit that God never called me to be somebody else. God called me to be Mel Holder! I suddenly realized that everything I needed in order for me to be Mel Holder had already been provided. Without realizing it I had been traveling in the wrong lane. My car had been sputtering and jerking around because the gasoline I had been putting into it was not the right octane. You see, no matter how much I practiced, I would simply never achieve the talent I wanted because it was just not in my DNA.

I quickly repented and began to develop the talents that God had graciously and unmistakably given to me. This resulted in launching a music ministry which to date has produced various multi-media products. More importantly it produced the climate wherein I could be a blessing to the body of Christ. Clearly I have found my lane by being faithful with the vehicle God has given me to drive.

The best advice I can offer you is to get into your own vehicle and fill it with passion, which is the gasoline that makes things happen. Then put the pedal to the metal and hit the road for God.

Fast Forward

†

What steps have you taken to find your lane?

†

What are some of the obstacles you have encountered while finding your lane?

NOTES

NOTES

CHAPTER THIRTEEN
~POSITIONING~

The golden rule of real estate is location, location, location. Being on a major boulevard or highway or in a popular mall rewards a business with much needed traffic. In the world of business promotion, this just-right "location" occurs when people have proven to be an asset instead of a liability. We are aware of this kind of positioning; however, I want to share with you how to position yourself in order for your talent to be matured and rewarded with God's promotion.

Your talent will open many doors for you and place you in a position to receive benefits that otherwise might not come along. We have a term for this principle. It is called the "Law of Attraction." Proverbs 18:16 declares that your gift will make room for you and bring you before great men.

This clearly means that your gift will bring you to the place where you can receive awesome opportunities in every aspect of your life -- financially, naturally, spiritually and emotionally.

From the age of fifteen I was on the road traveling as a musician. Even before I made a commitment to Christ, it was because of my talent that I was in position to be able to travel to see many cities of the world. Many of us may not have had the chance to experience such early opportunities and may feel a bit cheated. On the other hand, many who have had some level of success but now find themselves not in position for those experiences may become impatient. It is much like sitting at home, waiting for the phone to ring or an email to arrive with good news about a job or an opportunity, while watching everyone around you seemingly getting ahead.

The best way to describe positioning is to be where God wants when He wants you there. When we are not in the right place we are out of position and are prone to making mistakes. That is why it is the duty of every believer to be spiritually employed. Find a position somewhere and get busy for God. You may want to start right in the local church. The local church always has a need for good people who can operate with a servant's heart. Doing this has great rewards and will position you to be a blessing to the Body of Christ and the world.

*"Your first priority should always be
To position yourself in God's Word."*

Evidence that we have properly positioned ourselves in a committed relationship to Christ is seen when everyone involved is practicing and walking in sound biblical principles. This is a fundamental mandate for serving God. We get off track when we lose our reasoning ability and suddenly feel it's time to take matters into our own hands, instead of staying on track and trusting and waiting on God. All that we will accomplish in this mode is being driven by selfish motivation instead of being guided by the Holy Spirit.

When you operate selfishly, you unwittingly give permission to your flesh to rule over your decisions and actions. When you are operating in the flesh, you will find yourself doing things to please the flesh. I must warn you. Once the flesh is being pleased, it is never satisfied. It always craves more and more, which then leads to the emphasis being on "I". Out of "I" comes the operation of ego. Ego is the "I" of self importance in a person's mind, will and emotions. Ego's twin is Pride, and pride is the predecessor to destruction. The moral of this is, when we operate out of ego and pride, we position ourselves for a fall, the same way Satan did.

Satan was perfect in his form, and his bearing was noble and majestic. He had a special light that beamed from his countenance and shone all around him, brighter and more beautiful than any of the other angels. He was one with the Father before the angels were created. With all this stature and position, it was still Christ, God's dear Son, who had the pre-eminence over the entire angelic host.

At some point Satan became envious of Christ and gradually found his ego and pride so enlarged that they placed him in the position to lose everything. That is why it is so important as creative people to understand how being in the wrong place will birth the spirit of pride and rebellion which will in turn cost us everything.

When the spirit of pride and rebellion infiltrates our spirit, it brings us down just as it did Satan. Let's face it, as artists and performers we tend to get a great deal of praise and accolades. Our skills, talents and abilities are often celebrated in abundance, and in many cases this adoration and praise create a false sense of greatness. If this is not balanced by the Holy Spirit, we are certainly positioning ourselves for a fall.

"When the focus is not upward we are destined to fall"

A final key ingredient in properly positioning yourself for promotion is to allow the Spirit of God to fill you every day, so you can operate under God's power and anointing. If you fail to do so, you may find yourself operating in another attribute of the Luciferian Spirit, the spirit of division. When egos are not subjected to the Holy Spirit, the stage is set for division to happen. Just one musician or singer in the band or praise team can create an atmosphere of division. All it takes is one angry word between two people and unity is lost. That is why it is so very important to keep the peace no matter what it costs. The rewards are unlimited and innumerable.

Let me encourage you to position yourself so you can be a conduit for His presence. Let your actions and words be positive and uplifting. Walk worthy of your calling, understanding that when you are in the right position, you can achieve things that can literally change the course of history.

Fast Forward:

†

How are you currently positioning yourself to be a blessing to the body of Christ?

†

What is the Holy Spirit doing in your life to bring balance?

NOTES

CHAPTER FOURTEEN
~PREP WORK~

"Your preparation is a conversation with God."

In every vocation there is a season of preparation before a person actually engages in a certain field of expertise. Unless you formally study and pass all your tests, it is impossible to graduate, much less graduate with honors. This same principle applies to the kingdom of God. It was Paul the Apostle who contended with Silas regarding young Timothy as to whether or not he was seasoned enough to travel with them. In the end Timothy would come to be the spiritual son of Paul and go on to write several of the books of the Bible.

His early years were not as illustrious, and he had to prove he was ready and worthy of serving alongside Paul.

Paul was not being egotistical by any means. He was simply aware of the conditions of the world where he was trying to reach with the message of Christ and wanted Timothy to be well prepared. The time that Timothy spent under Paul's mentorship was vital preparation for him. While under Paul's leadership he learned the nuances of evangelism and apostolic administration. This period of preparation lasted several years as he spent time traveling and learning. His apprenticeship was well worth it in the end.

No matter what occupation you choose, there is a learning curve attached to it. Some careers require graduate school while others require vast experience in the field. I cannot imagine anyone being a success just because he has his name on a business card. We must perform well in order to meet the expectations of our vocation, just as Timothy had to do with Paul.

Let's look at another application for the word 'preparation'. When I think of the term 'prep' I immediately think of a surgical setting. Long before the patient goes into surgery, the nurses prep them. Once the prep has been accomplished, the patient is then ready for the operating room and the surgeon. The many years of medical school training was the prep work for the nurses and the doctors. Only when they graduated and were qualified were they entrusted to practice medicine.

There is a common thread found between these two examples and it is the discipline of learning. While experience can be a great teacher, the classroom can provide an atmosphere where one can analyze and research the pros and cons of any situation. Once the student begins his career he will soon become aware of just how effective his prep work was. If he was diligent in his study, he will be rewarded with success. If he was lazy and did not study as he should have, he will fail and possibly lose his job. Knowledge is everything when it comes to one's vocation. God sees knowledge as a vital part of your development as a believer, and even much more as a creative artist.

"Preparation Develops Results"

Spending preparation time with God simply means we are preparing ourselves for service. We may not know the day or the hour when God will call on us to do something with our talent. We may not know which person God might use us to speak to or even the place where God wants us to serve unless we spend time with Him preparing to receive His instructions. If we are prepared, by keeping our hearts and minds open at all times, we will not miss any of these opportunities.

Let me share with you just one example of being prepared. Imagine being called to do an impromptu version of the national anthem at the local kindergarten graduation ceremony down the street. Don't you think you should prepare for it just as much as if you were called to render a live performance of the same song at the Super Bowl? Remember, it is important not only what we do for Christ, but also how we do it.

"Practice and repetition are essential...
If we plan to develop and grow."

So, how do we develop and grow? The answer is practice, plain and simple. We will never reach our potential unless we are willing to put the time in preparation and practice.

What practice means is repeating actions over and over again until they become second nature or you master them. Time waits for no man. If you are not preparing yourself for the challenges ahead, you will quickly come face to face with the challenge and lose the battle. If someone else is out there with less talent but is applying the time and making the necessary sacrifices, he will win over the person who might have greater talent but has not spent time preparing. The person with less talent will win because he prepared better.

"Preparation Leads To Discoveries And Creativity."

You will learn some very valuable lessons about yourself while in preparation. And one of those lessons will deal with commitment. The genuine test of commitment is action. If you aspire to be a great musician and never practice, there is no commitment! It's just talk. When you diligently prepare by investing hours of practice, you affirm your commitment. Every time you follow through on your commitment, that follow-through fortifies your commitment until it is razor-sharp.

Preparation shows diligence. Diligence shows a readiness and willingness to improve. No matter where you find yourself today, your performance can always be improved. Lack of preparation reveals contentment and laziness. The great author Harvey Mackay said, "A good leader understands that anything that has been done in a particular way for a given amount of time is being done wrong. Every single performance can be improved."

With the introduction of the Internet we have access to numerous websites, which provide a wealth of information that can help us to develop and grow. If we utilize these sites, there is a good chance we will receive a much higher level of responsibility simply because we learned better ways to get a specific job done. Every one likes to see the finished product. No one really wants to go through the hours, days, weeks, months and even years it takes to produce a finished product. But once it is finished, there is no greater thrill than to unveil it for the world to see.

It takes diligence to take the seed which God has planted in you and allow Him to mature it. This seed will never grow just by virtue of its presence. Preparation is the water that stimulates its growth. Once growth is in process, you will encounter challenges and will most certainly make mistakes. Don't worry. Mistakes are part of growth and they will give you meaningful lessons that will lead you in the direction of reaching your peak performance. What is important is that you need to be in an environment where mistakes are allowed. Improvement always requires some degree of failure.

You must be able to prepare in an environment where experimentation and exploration are allowed. You may encounter periods of frustration during a season of failure and that is totally normal. However, the day you set your mind on ultimate success and get fed-up with failure is the day you become a winner.

"Preparation Develops Humility."

If there is one single lesson we all must learn before we successfully pass the test, it would be humility. Humility is not a character or personality trait that we were given at birth.

Humility is not being fearful and feeling puny either. Humility is the acknowledgment of our humanity while embracing the revelation that we are the children of God. Humility will bring about an ever present yearning to pursue. Humility embraces small beginnings with excitement and fervor. Dale Carnegie, one of the world's most famous human relations experts advised, "Don't be afraid to give your best to what seemingly are small jobs. Every time you conquer one it makes you that much stronger. If you do little things well the big ones tend to take care of themselves."

When you have made up your mind to prepare for your next level, never let the insignificant things block your progress. The proof of your desire is the intensity of your pursuit, and out of that pursuit you will experience growth. Step by step, one lesson after another is the process required for each of us to arrive at the destination marked "mature and ready." You will not need to announce your arrival or graduation. The simple fact that your gift and calling have increased under the tutelage of the Holy Spirit will be more than enough to cause everyone to celebrate with you regarding what God has done and is doing.

If I can leave you with one vital bit of information, I would choose to encourage you to begin today to prepare for the greatest adventure you will ever take. The more you seek Him, the more you will find Him. Once you find you are deeply engrossed in what He is doing and in turn practice in order to minister to Him, then you will suddenly wake up one morning and find your talent and gift have somehow fully blossomed into a marvelous gift for the world to experience.

*"There is always a price to pay…
To reach the final reward level."*

Fast Forward:

†

How have you disciplined yourself to be better prepared?

†

What valuable lessons have you learned about yourself while in preparation?

NOTES

CHAPTER FIFTEEN
~HINDRANCES~

"Your talent may take you far…
But it takes character and integrity to sustain it."

Talent will always attract attention, especially if it's outstanding or above average. Positive attention may place one in the position to be a part of a professional sports team or even to obtain a lucrative recording contract. The negative effect in most cases will come as subtle distractions, which may eventually hinder your success. They may come in the form of people who draw close to you because they lust after your talent. They can appear as groupies, supporters, aficionados or plain old fans. It is not unusual to find some of these folks going to extreme measures to show their gratitude. This may even appear in immoral sexual activities.

Another danger to this kind of adoration is when you start to believe the hype and begin to think more highly of yourself than you really should. Compliments are nice but be careful not to get caught up in them and lose sight of reality.

Talent is God-given so we should always walk in humility and thankfulness to God. Not being thankful is a selfish and fleshly attitude that can hinder our witness for Christ. Most of us in ministry would never think that we are operating out of our fleshly desires, but when we least expect it, sin can creep in subtly creating a mountain so big it hinders us from reaching our godly potential.

Look at Satan's desire for respect and recognition. Esteem and praise were motivators that drove his actions and duties. He was not concerned with how much glory God received but was driven by accomplishing his own personal goals and agendas. He used his gifting and talent as a means to manipulate attention to himself. His own pride became a hindrance to his position in the heavens. Now, let me bring this down to earth.

We would never blatantly confess to any of these actions but if we are totally honest with ourselves, we have all participated in these behaviors on some level. For instance, worship leaders have you ever extended worship beyond the allotted time because you felt you were in charge and had the right to do so? Musicians, have you consistently come late to rehearsals or not shown up at all because you felt that the rest of the team was wasting time? These types of behavior are hindrances.

In some cases it may not be that obvious but no matter what form it takes, it is quite destructive. It's like a cancer that is constantly growing in a dark corner of the body. Satan's plan is to destroy everything that God has placed in us. Satan wants us to walk in ignorance, which hinders us from operating in godly knowledge. He is the founding father of ignorance and he goes to great lengths to ensure we think that way. He is constantly in a state of war against the kingdom of God and the Body of Christ.

"We must operate with the knowledge of the Word of God to circumvent the attacks of Satan... even in their simplest form."

One of Satan's favorite hindrances is working with our pride. Pride always hinders us to the point where we believe we are "all that" and therefore it is not necessary for us to submit to and follow spiritual authority. If you refuse to respect and submit to those who have been placed in authority, you can become a hindrance.

Let's say you are supposed to be in choir rehearsal but you are nowhere to be found because you felt 'led' to go help out in the children's church. While it is not wrong to help the children's ministry, it is wrong if your commitment is to the choir as that is where you are supposed to be. To do otherwise is to create a hindrance to the success of the choir. I encountered a similar situation while serving with an individual who confronted me about my performance on a musical passage.

He did not like the way I was playing it. Even to this day I believe that I was playing the passage correctly. The issue was not about what I felt or my opinion. The issue was, I had to submit to his authority despite how I interpreted the situation.

He was the director and had the authority to make that call and decision. It was my place to accept his leadership. When he spoke to me in a rough tone that was callous, insensitive and loveless, my flesh became inflamed. I personally wanted to read him the riot act. I thought "Who does he think he is talking to?" This was clearly an issue where my flesh wanted to break out, but fortunately I did not allow my flesh to get the best of me.

I suddenly heard God say to me that I should hold my peace and that He had my back. I also heard the Lord say to me that I should humble myself under the mighty hand of God, that He may exalt me in due season. Even though my ego and pride were bruised, I felt a peace that was from the Holy Spirit. I suddenly realized this was a test and I knew I had passed with flying colors. From this situation I learned a very valuable lesson.

Obedience is better than sacrifice and it is always better to be a blessing than a hindrance.

You may have experienced similar situations where you had to overcome your fleshly desire to react. You may have felt that you were more talented or gifted than those who had delegated authority over you. The test you were facing was to see how you would respond. If you responded with subtle defiance, you were a hindrance. When someone has been given authority, we all must recognize their position and work within that framework.

For example if you are a worship leader doing your own thing and not following the instructions of your pastor, you are a hindrance. If you are a choir member not adhering to dress codes, you are a hindrance. If you are a musician playing too loud, over playing or playing out of tune, you are a hindrance. You are a hindrance if you are in leadership and you refuse to submit to those over you and then turn around and attempt to have people follow after you. These may seem to be small hindrances however; the enemy uses these and many other devious devices to hinder the Body of Christ.

It is important to understand that Satan prefers to isolate us to the point where we feel we should be in control. More often than not Satan seeks to manipulate those already unhappy with leadership. In some ways Satan's hindering spirit seeks out those who are sympathetic to its opinions and infects them through subversive methods. Satan is subtle and those who are being influenced by him rarely realize it until it's too late.

Masking sincere concern and making sarcastic comments are the personality of Satan's hindering spirit. Rarely will people go directly to the pastor with their problems because they think the pastor is their problem. They seek to validate their rebellion by gaining the support of those around them, causing anyone who agrees with them to be hindered in their walk with Christ. If you find yourself operating in any of these hindrances, repent immediately!

*"We are an extension of God's glory...
Our purpose is to exalt and worship Him."*

Satan's plan is to hinder our praise and worship to God. That is why he does his best to create hindrances on any level. If he can accomplish disrupting praise and worship, he will consider that he has done his job. Our plan should be to thwart his plan by implementing God's plan! God's plan is for us to allow Him to fight our battles while we praise and worship Him. To allow ourselves to wallow in ignorance and rebellion while the enemy triumphs over us is deplorable. We were created for wisdom not ignorance. We were created for victory and not defeat. We have the mind of Christ and when we worship and praise Him, we are declaring victory over Satan's hindrances.

> *"Wisdom is the ability to apply knowledge.*
> *Understanding is the ability to apply…*
> *Both wisdom and knowledge."*

Fast Forward:
†
What can you do to prevent hindrances
in your walk with Christ?
†
What should you do when you find a person on your team
becoming a hindrance?

NOTES

NOTES

CHAPTER SIXTEEN
~CHOICES~

God's purpose, plan and call for your life are not a guessing game or a multiple choice question on a test, yet we all have to make choices each and every day. These choices will always reveal who we really are, where we are going and how we are going to get there. God invites us to tune in to His station and listen attentively to His frequency where we will get guidance on making the right choices for our life.

The reason why we make bad choices is because we get bad reception or no reception at all due to obstacles and distractions that are blocking the signal. Clear your environment of anything that takes your attention away from God and keeps you from making the right choices.

More importantly, do an inventory of your relationships as they are either driving you towards God or they are taking you away from God. It's not just the big things that are the distractions, many times it's the little things that seem so innocent yet pull us away from the plan and purpose for our lives.

> *"Many of us miss God in the ordinary because we look for Him only in the extraordinary."*

Once these things are under control the path is clear to hear from God. God uses the simple things to reveal himself to us. Staying focused in the Word of God creates a deep conviction and assurance that you are walking in God's divine plan and purpose for your life. You have to realize that when God created you He threw away the mold and that He has a unique recipe for your success. Remember, we should become imitators of Christ and allow the good works of our fellow brethren to inspire us towards Christ.

I have personally come to know some of the finest jazz musicians who are also strong Christians. They are out in their part of the vineyard doing a secular job yet still representing Christ. Now I know that there are many Christians who subscribe to the fact that you cannot play secular music and still walk with Christ. My response is a candid comment, "What Would Jesus Do (WWJD)?" Remember, for the first thirty years of Jesus' life He occupied Himself with secular matters before He launched His public ministry. For almost half of His life His vocation was that of a carpenter.

I would like to ask you to consider with me for a few moments the significance of the fact that Jesus Christ served as a carpenter actually much longer than He ever served in His public ministry. The fact that He was a carpenter for those 15 years emphasizes the fact that God respects all honorable work that we might do, even manual labor as a carpenter would have been engaged in. This shows the humility of Jesus as He was in preparation for His calling and ministry. Just as Christ was certain to have done, your understanding God's period of preparation will give you the experience needed to function in capacities that may or may not be glamorous. This is all in the process of our development which guides us to our calling.

> *"It's important that we take our gifts and use them to influence the cause of Christ in the secular arena."*

As creative artists and Christians we are the salt of the earth; therefore, we need to represent the gospel of Jesus Christ wherever we find ourselves. I strongly believe that if you are working in a secular environment that it is important to remain rooted and grounded in the Word and surround yourself with strong Christian fellowship. You cannot survive out there without these elements because if you are not effecting a change in your environment, then your environment will change you. Let me give an example of what can happen when you begin to follow Christ in a secular setting.

When I accepted Christ in my life I was playing in a secular band which was out on the road traveling from city to city. My first encounter with the band after accepting Jesus in my life was quite interesting because I no longer had the appetite or the desire to do the things that were associated with being a musician on the road.

I remember clearly one incident when we were up in Boston doing some shows. We were scheduled to do two shows a night and the first night out the venue was packed to the brim. So the promoter decided that he would add a third show. However, my contract clearly stated to do two shows, and I felt it was not prudent for me to do an additional show as a young Christian. I told them that I would honor my contractual commitment but I was not going to do an additional performance. This did not sit well with management and I was fired from the group.

Now by no means am I saying this is the path for every Christian artist, but for me it was essential to make a firm stand as to what was right or wrong for me. After leaving the group I came to realize that God wanted me to have that time of separation so I could get to know who He was and understand my calling in Him.

The most important factor was for me to know God and know who I was in Him. When you are an artist you are faced with all these elements of both the church and the secular environment. How we handle our witness in both of these areas is the real test. If we choose to follow Christ, the proof will be seen by everyone, especially Him. Make sure every choice you make would be the same choice Jesus would make.

Fast Forward:
†
Can you pinpoint the choice that ushered you into your calling?
†
Have you continued to nurture the decision or have you allowed the materialism of this world to snuff it out?

NOTES

NOTES

CHAPTER SEVENTEEN
~FAITHFULNESS~

In our society today, it is not difficult to spot and find talent. To find someone who is talented and faithful, however, is a tall order. Faithfulness like focus, which we discussed earlier, is not a God-given talent. Faithfulness must be developed and proven. You see it's easy to be faithful to your call when you are doing things that are pleasurable with people whom you enjoy being around. The true test of faithfulness is honoring your commitment in the midst of a challenging situation. Faithfulness is a paramount prerequisite for the total fulfillment of the call of God on your life. One of the first steps to develop faithfulness is to be conscientious and diligent in all that you do.

"True faithfulness is doing a task despite circumstances."

There are many types of situations we will face. Some are God sent and some are of our design. These events that God divinely sends to us are for the purpose of developing our character. Then there are events that God sends that are instrumental in teaching us a valuable lesson. God is always seeking people who are more than just gifted, but available.

As creative artists we tend to glory in our talents and gravitate towards the spotlight and the things that are grandiose, or at least they are in our minds. When you begin to demonstrate faithfulness in the small things that are not glamorous, God will trust you with more valuable opportunities.

In God's math the level of your commitment and faithfulness will always multiply your elevation. It pleases the heart of God when we are faithful servants and understand that our lives can be a tremendous blessing to our current society. The only way to accomplish this is to constantly walk and live our lives 'In Christ.' The way to be first is to be last and the way to be exalted is through humility. That may sound like a very simple statement but the demand it places on each of us can often seem overwhelming.

There is no better example of this than in the life of Christ when He was walking in the call and purpose of His earthly ministry. The things that we do out of love, even when it hurts to do them measure our faithfulness. Jesus was the personification of that act of unmeasured love. You see, you can do without love but you cannot love without doing. Many of us can relate to being faithful in situations where we are not appreciated or even tolerated but despite all of that, we still have a task and an assignment to accomplish. God honors faithfulness with great rewards when we persevere through the drama of life. God will order your steps and guide you through difficult times because He knows that we need His help.

Remember earlier I shared with you how unique man is because God gave him the power to create? When God spoke the worlds into existence He did so with words. Each day of creation began with God speaking three words before He said what He wanted to create. Those three words were "Let there be!" There is power in God's voice and the instant we became His children and allowed Him to make us a new creation, we were given His voiceprint. Before we became children of God, we could speak to situations and nothing would happen. Now that we are His children we have the power and right to speak and expect change!

You have to be very careful what you say, for life and death are in the power of the tongue. When you find yourself in a difficult situation and you begin to speak negatively, you create a negative climate and atmosphere. When you speak positive words you create a positive climate and atmosphere. There is a translation of the Bible entitled "God's Word" that has interpreted Proverbs 18:21 to read in this way; "The tongue has the power of life and death, and those who love to talk will have to eat their own words."

Wherever you go and whatever you are doing, God wants you to shine like a beacon of light so that the whole world can see Him in you. What makes this so hard to do is that it takes discipline to overcome our flesh. We are often too quick to judge situations and before we know it we are speaking negatively. Some situations can be toxic and require a deep level of prayer and consecration to overcome. Remember God always has your back and

He is still working on your behalf for your good. Where change is necessary and change does not occur, you will find the potential for destruction.

You should never stay in an environment where your weaknesses are magnified. If you are in a situation that is conflictive, where there seems to be a constant battle to resolve the issues, and you see no change or progress even after a substantial period of time, you must move on.

Being aware of the in-dwelling presence of the Holy Spirit is another way to develop faithfulness. The Holy Spirit will place into you a revelation concerning those insights He wants you to have. God will allow you to see things for your protection and for the purpose of applying proper protocol for ministry. You see, every problem on the surface is a problem of the heart. Any problem of the heart cannot be resolved on the surface.

"The heart holds the condition of everyone's walk."

Any success or failure is based on the approach. When God calls you to do something, the method you use to accomplish it is very important. We see many Christians who are hurt and derailed because of someone's approach to what they believe God was calling them to do. Meekness and humility are necessary for us to serve His people. If there is any one characteristic or attribute that causes a person to stand out in God's eyes, it is faithfulness. Faithfulness will cause someone to stand out from the crowd and be recognized on a higher level. When God finds someone who stays the course and is faithful and committed to his call, come hell or high water, he gets His undivided attention.

"As creative artists it is crucial that we make it our uttermost desire to develop the spirit of faithfulness "

We can see that faithfulness on the part of a Christian produces great joy and a victorious life as its end result. It is clear and definite that during the process you will experience battles and struggles. Jesus said throughout scripture that the things He did were to please His Father. In other words, Jesus was always faithful, even when He was tempted. It should be our heart's desire as Christians to please our heavenly Father in everything that we do. It is only through our faithfulness that we can ever hope to accomplish God's best and fulfill the height of our calling. It's not about how much we achieve materially in this life, but it's about whether we are moving forward towards maximizing our call, which will eventually affect the lives we encounter.

This all may seem very practical and easy when everything is going well and correctly. However, there will come a time when your faith and faithfulness will be tested. It may come in the area of finances, health, relationships or even a direct attack on your reputation. Your dedication to faithfulness comes through longsuffering, and everyone eventually endures levels of great hardship while walking with God. You need to be focused. We must concentrate on the task at hand in order to survive those seasons where there is an apparent lack of focus. If we are not careful, the things of the world will lead us away from the Lord through distractions and temptations.

We need to be devoted. Our devotion as Christians will strengthen us through the challenges of life. I remember some time back while in a church staff meeting that the pastor asked a staff member what he would do if the ministry could no longer pay him for his services. Could he still remain faithful to his calling? Here was this staff member's reply. He said; "The first thing I would do is to pray and seek God's guidance and wisdom in this situation. Then I would go and seek full time employment to take care of my family. After that was taken care of I would then volunteer my time and continue to be faithful to my service to God." This staff member demonstrated the three pertinent attributes of faithfulness; Long-suffering, Focus and Devotion.

We should all have the same humble spirit as this person exhibited. The local church or even your employer is not your source. God is. While we are required to be faithful in the marketplace, we are equally held accountable for our service to God. Abraham was faithful and it was accounted unto him as righteousness. God will reward you not only with His righteousness but also with many natural and spiritual blessings beyond your natural comprehension.

Fast Forward:
†
What can you do to take your faithfulness
to the next level?
†
Are there any distractions in your life that are
preventing you from being faithful?

NOTES

NOTES

CHAPTER EIGHTEEN
~CORPORATE SERVICE~

*"Singers, musicians, dancers and actors who serve
God's people have to realize that it takes
more than talent to serve God with your gift."*

Imagine for a moment that you have arrived at the church for choir rehearsal. All day long you have been looking forward to the new song you are learning. You find your spot in your section that is standing next to someone who is your elder in the Lord and just happens to be 68 years old. This individual struggles with being able to focus on her part and no matter how hard she tries, she continues to sing the wrong note. This has been an ongoing problem and you have done your best to help her in the past by making CD's of her vocal line so she can rehearse at home. You have done your best to assist her and continue to show patience.

The rehearsal continues and suddenly a fellow choir member in the row in front of you looks back at the elder vocalist and a bit too loudly says, "Hey what are you doing back there? You are singing flat!" You, along with others, are stunned in disbelief that someone would react in such a rude and robust manner, especially after praying just five minutes earlier. Your flesh is burning to respond to his lack of sensitivity and your spirit man is pouring cold water on you as fast as it can. What an embarrassing situation!

What you have just read is just one of the universal sound bites that can be found in choirs, bands and numerous creative arts departments all over the world. No matter what the setting, this type of behavior is just not acceptable. First, and foremost, it creates an uncomfortable atmosphere for everyone, not to mention how it makes the recipient feel. Unless the person making the statement apologizes, there will continue to be a rift in the unity of the entire group.

Let me explain. When someone makes a comment like this, there will always be those who will agree with them because they feel superior. Then there are those who will side with the person to whom the comment is addressed. The end result is that the unity is broken and the choir is divided, all because of one person's comment.

There are many who will take advantage of these types of uncomfortable situations and use them as excuses to stay away from a corporate environment. When we take the attitude that we can make it all by our self and feel we don't need to come to the house of God to be disrespected, we are the ones who lose. Feeling that way in the natural may have some merit to it, but the end result is the same. We end up being disconnected.

When you walk in the Spirit, you have to choose not to let these emotions hinder you. Although it is painful to go through these tense moments, they do offer us an opportunity to grow and become victorious in even the most undesirable of situations.

Sometimes growth can only take place completely in a structured setting like a school or even in an informal setting like playing in a local basement or garage band. The common thread in all these settings is that they all involve groups of people. If we were honest about it, we would admit that it is difficult to master being in a choir, band or play when we never interact with the other members.

Let me give you an example. Imagine being asked to play at the Presidential Inauguration with a group of musicians you have never played with. They send you the rehearsal tapes and tell you the time and place for the performance. That is the good news. The bad news is that there will be no rehearsal! You will not have any time to get together with the other musicians and go over the charts and rehearse. The entire performance will be off the cuff. It sounds ridiculous doesn't it?

The truth is that while it could be done, there is an even better chance that its result could possibly turn out to be a massive embarrassment for everyone.

Here again, interaction with others in a corporate setting is essential to excellence in service. As you personally develop, you will find a great benefit to various types of interaction which can come only from a corporate setting. This setting is generally serving with others who share your same passion. You will usually find this environment in the local church which provides a corporate setting for us to serve, develop and grow.

Your involvement in the ministries of the local church will allow you the time and experience to learn three basic purposes.

The first of these basic purposes is the opportunity to share your gift with others as an offering of corporate worship back to God. The second basic purpose is to learn and develop ministry skills. The third basic purpose is to present your service on a global platform as a part of the universal Body of Christ.

Even if you believe that your calling is that of a solo artist, it is imperative that you spend time going through these three phases so that you can mature. God grants a personal anointing to individuals who develop their personal skills, as we have seen in the parable of the talents. God also grants a corporate anointing over us as we serve in our local churches and then ultimately to the worldwide Body of Christ. Every single artist, singer, musician, and dancer needs the benefit of a corporate setting to grow, mature and develop in. If you are not currently serving in a local church, go into prayer and earnestly ask God to guide you to a place where you can grow and develop while also being a blessing to others as you serve God.

Once you have found a place, then it's time to go to work. Bear in mind that the place where God calls you to serve is the place where you can discover a deep joy, even while you are being stretched to reach the next level of your development. At times it will not be a comfortable place, but in the end it will always be a rewarding place. Never mistake comfort as a prerequisite for being in the right setting for growth and maturity.

All too often we will discover that being in uncomfortable settings can place a demand on our character and in turn create a maturity that cannot be produced in an unchallenging situation. Sometimes a challenge is the best catalyst to successful service to the kingdom of God. It is important for us to realize that we are a part of something much greater than ourselves.

The outcome of our endeavors, both individually and corporately, may not be seen immediately, if ever. We may never know all the testimonies of people who have been healed and delivered while experiencing a corporate worship setting. I cannot express to you how important it is that we understand that our worship services are many times evangelical in their impact. As creative artists in the local church, we share in the office of evangelists by declaring the 'good news' through our talents and gifts.

Godly service always creates a global outreach which extends far beyond the walls of our local church. Once the local church is empowered with unity to serve, the community will begin to make comments about how important their presence is among them. The Word of God says they will know us by our love for the brethren. It also states that we are written epistles, known and read of all men. What we do, say, sing and play is being watched. Our service is being looked at with great interest.

I pray you will see the value of becoming a positive influence in the corporate setting you presently serve in.

Fast Forward:
†
What can you do to avoid conflict and promote a peaceful atmosphere for serving?
†
What challenges are you currently facing at your house of worship?

NOTES

NOTES

CHAPTER NINETEEN
~LAW AND ORDER~

Imagine yourself out for a drive. You are enjoying a beautiful day in the Lord and your vehicle's audio system is operating in full effect. You hit the preset button and suddenly the environment is filled with the sounds of Kirk Franklin; you hit the preset button again and there is a brilliant T.D. Jakes sermon electrifying the atmosphere. You might choose to hit the preset once more, only to be engaged by an instrumental praise by yours truly, Mel Holder. Thank you very much!

Suddenly the sound of a siren takes you from the pleasure of your inspirational moment. You quickly glance at your rear view mirror only to see flashing lights commanding your attention. Without hesitation you pull your vehicle to the side of the road – obeying the law. As you wait quietly in your vehicle, you hear the sound of a car door opening and closing and then the sound of boots against the pavement. The next few seconds seem like hours, as if each one is unfolding in slow motion.

The short distance from the patrolman's car to yours seems like a country mile. The officer finally arrives at your window and you greet him with respectful pleasantries. "Good day, Officer." He barely acknowledges you and firmly asks for your license and registration. He then asks you the one question you do not want to hear, "Do you know how fast you were going?" You dodge the question. "Officer, I hardly ever speed."

Despite the fact that most of the time you obey the law, this time you did not. Now you find yourself in a situation where you must pay for your disobedience. It does not matter that ninety-nine times prior to this situation you were in total compliance with the law. The fact is, this time you got caught!

"We are not rewarded for obeying the law…
Obedience is our obligation."

I can almost hear you asking to yourself; "What does this have to do with my pursuit of my creative calling?" I am glad you asked.

I used this illustration to emphasize the fact that too often we get caught up in the moment and don't realize what is going on around us. When we get distracted and take our eyes off the speedometer which, in this case, is the Word of God, we are likely to speed. And speeding is breaking the law, even if it is not done intentionally.

As creative people, we are easily caught up in what it is that we are doing instead of realizing we are a part of something much bigger than ourselves. We get caught up in who we are, who we know and what we have done, and before we know it we are going one hundred miles an hour down a highway headed for a wreck. Laws are put in place to protect us and help us to avoid wrecks. God will always place someone in our life to operate in the same capacity as that law enforcement officer. This is usually done to get our attention.

> *"For rulers are not a terror to good works, but to the evil. Wilt thou then not be afraid of the power? Do that which is good, and thou shalt have praise of the same: for he is the minister of God to thee for good."*
> Romans 13:3,4

These confrontations are never easy and can even be traumatic. Our spirit man does not like to be chastised for the same reason that our natural man does not like to be confronted, challenged or corrected.

> *"Now no chastening for the present seemeth to be joyous, but grievous: nevertheless afterward it yieldeth the peaceable fruit of righteousness unto them which are exercised thereby."* Hebrews 12:11

Now imagine that your court date has arrived and you are sitting in a court of law, listening to lawyers' debate as to whether you should or should not be punished for speeding. Behind the judge is a picture of Lady Justice, the personification of truth and fairness. She is blindfolded so that who or what she sees cannot influence her. She listens and holds in her hands a scale where arguments for and against you are placed.

If there is enough evidence that says you are innocent, you will go free. If there is more evidence that proves you did the crime you will be sentenced and punished. Lady Justice never sees your face. All she listens for is truth. When she hears enough she will make a fair decision. You know the truth.

Natural truths mirror spiritual truths. We have traffic laws to prevent chaos. These laws actually protect us -- when they are obeyed. There are similar laws in operation when it comes to our spiritual lives. These laws have a direct impact on our gifting and calling.

As I stated in Chapter Two, our calling is a vehicle, which is powered by our passion. While we may feel that our passion is pure, there are times that our vehicle may get out of control because we gave our vehicle, which is our calling, too much gasoline or passion.

God did not invest His love and power in your life just so you can be out of control and wreck everything. He has purposed that you should achieve exactly what He planned for you long before the foundation of the earth was even laid. He knows *"the thoughts that [He thinks] toward you… thoughts of peace, and not of evil, to give you an expected end"* (Jeremiah 29:11). You are not a mistake!

You are a child of divine destiny. You are a vehicle that has been created to carry the glory of God. The Holy Spirit will serve as your Godly Positioning System so that you will stay on course and not veer off the track. Your completion of this race is vital to your eternal destiny. It is not enough for you to be talented, gifted, anointed and recognized. Obeying the laws of the Spirit is vital to your goal of being a blessing to the Body of Christ. When the Spirit of God leads you, you will not have to worry about being arrested for breaking His commandments and laws.

Fast Forward:

†

When was the last time you were stopped for spiritual speeding?

†

Identify the person or persons in the natural who God has used to hold you accountable?

NOTES

CHAPTER TWENTY
~SHOW ME THE MONEY~

If you turn on the TV, radio or surf the internet, it is glaringly apparent that the pursuit of financial wealth is among the top five hottest topics. Huge mansions, exotic cars, designer clothes and diamond studded jewelry have replaced the American Dream of having a nice home and a family.

People struggle with working for minimum wage because it is virtually impossible to live on that amount of money. With all the economic pressures, not to mention the rising cost of living, the average individual now works more than one job and still continues to live from pay check to pay check.

When the phrase 'show me the money' first appeared in the movie, Jerry Maguire, starring Tom Cruise it was immediately a popular commentary among the American culture. Those four words became the battle cry of the working class. What they were actually saying was if you want someone to do a good job then pay the laborer a reasonable amount of money for doing it. Today, those words have taken on a completely different kind of meaning, especially in the realm of the church.

Despite how unholy, worldly or secular this chapter title may appear, there are a great many musicians, singers, artists and preachers who could be found guilty of being obsessed with money. One of the circumstances that leads to this is, disappointing situations that changed the way money is perceived. In some cases, these individuals were actually lied to and robbed by persons operating under the banner of ministry.

In other cases, they were consumed by their own desires and lust. No matter what the reason is, there is something wrong with being consumed with accumulating large sums of money in the name of God. Please don't get me wrong there is nothing wrong with honestly working to earn a living. God encourages us to use our creativity as an investment that pays dividends.

I have found two schools of thought when it comes to compensation to those in spiritual leadership. The first thought process is; churches that believe the creative arts are a serving ministry and should be administered by volunteers. They believe that there will always be someone available who is willing to direct, sing and play the instruments as a tithe to God. Their expectations are that each parishioner has the responsibilities and obligation to offer his time and talents to the church. They don't pay the Sunday school teachers, elders or deacons. These people are all volunteers who invest at least as many hours a week as the creative arts staff.

The second thought pattern can be found in churches that put a premium on their creative art department. They are willing to compensate financially their creative staff because they understand the importance of having a professional music department. Generally these often larger churches employ choral and instrumental arrangers on their music staff because they do a wide variety of music which requires a high level of skill.

The creative arts budget is significant in order to make certain that they are able to maintain highly talented individuals. Some even produce recordings and charge admission for a concert series to establish suitable levels of income. Not only is a director hired, but also several musicians and choir members are hired to assist, particularly for demanding music that accompanies special event productions, as well as the standard weekly music.

Today we find many churches with a balanced insight and understand the passage "a workman is worthy of his hire" and that its application is not limited to the preaching staff alone. One thing that should be understood is that when a person is paid, the church has a right to expect a higher level of commitment. This higher level of commitment should include creative individuals who have significant years of experience and training. These individuals are qualified to receive fair compensation for their services.

The church should have the benefit of talented persons who have prepared themselves naturally and spiritually for ministry. Anyone who believes he is called to an office should understand that God expects him to exhibit excellence in stewardship. Money should not be the motivation when it comes to ministry. What should be our motivation is the desire to use our talents to magnify Christ. When you are called to serve in a local church, your passion should be focused on getting the work of the Lord accomplished, not on money!. Money follows ministry, when ministry is following money we have totally missed the purpose of service.

Your time of service, in most cases, will usually far exceed the financial compensation. There is a deep contentment that comes from being obedient to God and serving His people. When our heart is in the right place, God will always provide the much needed provision. I feel I need to warn you that if you do any job half heartedly, it will not make anyone happy, including you!

Allow me to share something that I believe is an area that needs some attention. I have witnessed situations where musicians were running up to the stage to play after the Praise and Worship had already started. I am not saying that you can't be occasionally late; however, this practice is truly disrespectful to God and His people. You will never find a professional baseball, football, or basketball player running onto the court or field from the street five minutes after the game started. In professional sports athletes are required to be there three to four hours before the game actually begins. Their work day actually starts from that time of preparation hours before the game.

Consider this, if this is demanded and required in professional sports, there should be no difference in the house of God.

*"God's Kingdom should be a presentation…
of order, unity and discipline."*

I challenge my fellow creative artists not to become "Spiritual Free Agents" and seek to render your talents to the highest bidder. Allow God to plant you in the right ministry and avoid becoming a hireling. When you are driven solely by money, you will miss the essence of what God has for you. Remember as you serve in the local church, God will bring the increase! Nothing done in His name will ever go unrewarded.

Trust me, I know, I have been personally rewarded under this principle.

Remember that it is ultimately God who is your source. Those who reward you are God used vessels. Be faithful in your service, if you are serving at a local church honor the rules and regulations. Some of these regulations may require church membership and other prerequisites before you can actively serve on the staff or as a part of its auxiliaries and ministries. This practice has become quite poplar in recent times, especially with the emergence of mega-churches across the country.

This practice is very necessary for creative artists to develop their character as well as their spiritual and natural gifts.

In summation, let me bring this chapter to a close by asking you to take inventory of your motives for ministry. Are you in it for souls and to fulfill the mandate God has placed on your life, or have you been seduced into thinking that wealth is available to those in ministry? There is nothing wrong with the fact that there is provision in the position, but to make the position about the provision is definitely wrong.

Think of it this way. If you asked God to show you the money, how long do you think it would take for Him to show it all to you? He owns the gold and the silver and everything else! He also says that He will meet your need. He also promises that He will not withhold any good thing from His children. All of these declarations from God release us from being bound by the pursuit of money in order that we may pursue Him.

Fast Forward:
†
If your ministry could not afford to pay you,
would you still serve?
†
What are you currently doing at your house of worship
that demonstrates your commitment?

NOTES

YOUNG MEL

HAWAII

LONDON

BRAZIL

*"I waited patiently for the LORD;
and he inclined unto me, and heard my cry.*

*He brought me up also out of an horrible pit,
out of the miry clay, and set my feet upon a rock,
and established my goings.*

*And he hath put a new song in my mouth,
even praise unto our God: many shall see it,
and fear, and shall trust in the LORD."*

Psalm 40:1-3

CHAPTER TWENTY-ONE
~RELATIONSHIPS~

Has it ever occurred to you just how much we all depend on one another? We interact with people all day long in one way or another and when you think about it, our lives would be empty without somebody to talk to. This need to communicate is the reason God created mankind. Our creation was not because God was lonely. It was part of His master plan! We were not created as some afterthought. We were created with purpose. That purpose was to interact with our Creator. When God created mankind He did so by using the common denominator of two.

By choosing a man and a woman He established the significance of a relationship between two created beings. He knew that it would not be good for man to be alone so He gave him a companion, a helpmeet, a woman. God also knew that Adam could get much more accomplished with Eve at his side than he could all by himself. As human beings we crave the desire for understanding, affirmation and relationships. It's through these meaningful connections that we can experience these things.

One of the first ministry lessons I learned was the power of relationships. I have learned the importance of developing long lasting relationships as I traveled the world for the past fifteen years. Relationships have proven to be a very precious commodity, so much so that I value relationships over tangible resources any day. I have never seen anyone who has received any tangible item without its being tied to some kind of relationship whether natural or spiritual.

In my ministry there was not one opportunity that came my way that was not linked to a prior relationship. It became quite evident to me that it was not about what I knew professionally but who I knew personally and spiritually. Relationships serve a purpose and can span a lifetime or last for a limited season. Others may even hit a few snags that raise a red flag that says it's time to move on. All in all, relationships are paramount to having an encounter of productive impact while serving in your ministry.

"Gratitude confirms relationships."

One of the key elements of maintaining a relationship is the simple act of saying "thank you." These two words will benefit both the recipient and the person who says them. Expressing gratitude will improve your attitude toward people you serve or serve you. Gratitude strengthens relationships by causing the person expressing thanks to feel more responsible and committed to the relationship. When you are committed to a relationship, you are focused on the good characteristics of that person, which helps you to see them in a positive light.

Gratitude serves as a bond in a relationship so that both parties can proceed to the place where they place a higher value on the relationship, and are willing to make sacrifices and to go the extra mile to protect it. One thing I have learned to put into practice from the start of my career is to always send thank you letters to every church, ministry or organization where I had the opportunity to share my gift. Most people verbally thank those who gave them large love gifts, but there is nothing better than receiving a thank you note in the mail. Even if I did not receive an honorarium, I still sent a letter of gratitude for the time I was able to spend with that ministry. When I began to faithfully practice this principle, I was blessed with a harvest of phone calls inviting me to come and minister.

I always try to keep in touch with people who have graciously granted me a ministry opportunity throughout the years. I have found that communicating with people at times when you are not seeking something in particular releases a freedom to the relationship. There will always be times when you will experience pitfalls in relationships due to one reason or another. Sometimes it is because of something you have done, intentionally or not. Other times the pitfall occurs due to circumstances completely out of your control. Life is full of ups and downs, surprises and realizations, so get used to it. Learn how to shake off the negative and focus on the positive.

A relationship will always become strained when individuals feel disrespected, devalued, and experience a breakdown in communication. When these issues present themselves, it is best to do all you can do to resolve them in a peaceful manner. Try having an honest and open conversation about your concerns, and if that doesn't work it may be time to go separate ways. When it's time to discontinue a relationship, do so prayerfully and don't burn your bridges. Make your exit in the most respectful manner possible. That means expressing your gratitude and speaking words of affirmation. How you leave one relationship will determine how you start the next one.

You may feel the need to review relationships you have encountered to see if you could have handled them better. Or you may now see how a relationship failed simply because of extrinsic problems neither person was responsible for. Cherish the relationships you are presently in and remember to share your appreciation and affirmation with your friends and associates now and not later. You will enjoy a much richer life, and so will they.

Fast Forward:
†
What can you do to strengthen and confirm your relationships in ministry?
†
What can you change in your personality to demonstrate a greater attitude of gratitude?

NOTES

NOTES

CHAPTER TWENTY-TWO
~OPTIONS~

By now it is clear that God gives talent to whomever He pleases. Man, in his limited mental capabilities, cannot come up with any comprehensive conclusion as to why or to whom God gives talent. Let's just say God has that right because He is God Almighty, the All Powerful King of Glory and the Everlasting Omniscient Creator. When you look at God from our viewpoint, it seems to not matter as much what He does or how He does it.

Remember, in an earlier chapter, I said that man is made in the image and likeness of God? We have one element that is unique to us--one characteristic that makes us different from the rest of creation. We have the ability to create. Evidence of this can be found everywhere on our planet.

Yes, we are fearfully and wonderfully made, and what we manifest using our talent is our doing--good or bad. We have the power to create because of God's creative gift to and in us.

William Jennings Bryan, the great Orator and Attorney, said, "Destiny is no matter of chance. It is a matter of choice: It is not a thing to be waited for, it is a thing to be achieved."

Our success or failure is completely dependent on what we do with the options and choices that are presented to us. It's those key decisions that separate us from others who operate on talent alone. When we choose our options, they should line up with our purpose and core values, and those choices must cost us something. David, an incredible worshipper, said, *"neither will I offer...unto the LORD my God of that which doth cost me nothing"* (2 Samuel 24:24). You cannot expect a free ride.

At a young age I realized that I had musical talent. I was fortunate enough to attend the Erasmus Hall Institute for Performing Arts in Brooklyn, New York. There was a curriculum designed to develop talent in gifted students in the Arts. I had to audition to get into the school and when I found out that I was accepted, I was truly excited.

When I got to the school, it did not take me long to realize that what talent I had was, at best, average. I thought back to the days when I was in junior high school. In those days, I was the best saxophonist in the class. I remembered being a part of the Borough-Wide Jazz Band and performing one of my first concerts at Carnegie Hall at the age of 13. I was astonished that at Erasmus Hall Institute I was just one of many talented musicians. You see what is outstanding on one level is average on a higher level.

I had an option at 15, whether I was going to accept average or work hard and develop my talent until it--*no*--I was exceptional. I chose to work hard and develop my talent. Once again I was fortunate enough to get a private teacher, and my weekly lessons helped me tremendously. By the time I reached my senior year at Erasmus Hall, I was at the top of my class.

I was in the very talented Erasmus High Jazz Band and I received many write-ups in the local newspapers for my accomplishments. That was all good, but soon it was time to go to college and again, I was presented with an option. At this new level my talent was again average, at best! I applied the same work ethic and even met with other talented musicians who influenced my growth. (Thanks to all you guys!)

I remember meeting Arthur Rhames. To this day, I believe Arthur was one of the most talented individuals to ever grace this planet. Arthur opened up a whole new world of music to me. He was a musical genius who had an ultra-disciplined practice routine. He inspired me to invest time into my talent. Arthur and I would practice for ten to twelve hours a day. He had an understanding of musical concepts that few could comprehend. He was so advanced that he has been given credit for creating the avant-garde jazz music scene.

No matter how many hours I practiced with Arthur, I could never do what he did. Yes, I got better. I improved tremendously. But I never rose to the level Arthur was on.

Then I realized that he was just more talented and gifted in his defined area. There were times that I got frustrated and wanted to give up because I could not perform on his level. Although I had not yet accepted the Lord into my life, I realized that I had to go about this thing entirely different. I had come face to face with the fact that I had to do things on another stage that would enable me to maximize my talent. That was a very valuable option.

The scriptures teach that we must *"run with patience the race that is set before us"* (Hebrews 12:1). I made the decision to run my race rather than fretting over not being able to catch Arthur. It was not long after I reached the glorious point in my life that I accepted the Lord Jesus Christ into my heart and life. To this day, I can testify that it was the best decision I ever made. That decision directed me to the place where my talent was to be planted. Yes, it was the choice I made which placed Jesus in my life and put me in what I call 'my zone.'

Arthur and I drifted away from each other due to my new found faith in Jesus Christ and Arthur's practices as a devotee of Hare Krishna. Almost a decade later, I found out that Arthur died at the age of 32. To this day, I still treasure the concepts and the musical training that I received from Arthur. I have come to the conclusion that my experiences and training with Arthur were specifically for that season of my life, and they were definitely God sent and God used.

You may find yourself in a place where you feel you are being left behind on the achievement curve. You may compare yourself to others and wonder how in the world you will ever achieve greatness with your 'average' talent. You may find yourself embarrassed by your lack of expertise. But I have some really great news for you.

Somewhere and sometime, when you least expect it, God will bring along a mentor who will unlock a new world to you. Being rooted and grounded in Christ will enhance the odds of that happening. "Be prepared" is always the best motto. There are many options that are presented to us on our journey. God has enabled us with the necessary tools to make the right decisions!

Fast Forward:
†
What options are currently in front of you?
†
Who has God placed in your life as an inspiration or mentor?

NOTES

CHAPTER TWENTY-THREE
~MAXIMIZING~

It's truly amazing to see how God has created mankind with each one having a different, unique, skill, talent, or ability which contributes to the total cultural make up of our planet. When God created each one of us, He had it in His mind for us to deposit something special into the world in which we live. Each individual, having his or her own unique talent, makes our planet a very interesting place. Out of all these skills, talents, and abilities, mankind has the distinction of having the greatest creative minds. As citizens of the planet Earth we all enjoy and benefit from the talent and creativity of each other.

We all benefit from the dreams that began in our ancestors and forefathers. These dreams, which at one time were mere ideas, now have grown into the massive technological advancements we enjoy today. What made these great achievements possible were the personal sacrifice and discipline of individuals who were willing to go beyond the norm to reach their highest potential. God has endowed each of us with an immeasurable treasure of talent, given to us for a divine purpose. Everything God has bestowed upon us has an intrinsic value and it's our responsibility to accept the challenge of birthing it.

It's very important for us to understand that maximizing our gift is not God's responsibility but is solely our own responsibility. The apostle Paul warned Timothy to *"Neglect not the gift that was in [him]"* (1 Timothy 1:14). He also warned the church at Philippi and us in the process to *"work out your own salvation with fear and trembling"* (Philippians 2:12).

We most certainly determine the degree to which our destiny and purpose get accomplished. How? We determine the measure of success in our lives through our willingness to cooperate with and follow God's assignment for our life. Even the most extraordinarily gifted and talented individual must have the inward drive and discipline to take that gift to the next level. We can look right into our own churches and see some of the most talented individuals who never reached the apex of their potential.

One day while I was on a video shoot at the cemetery where my father is buried, I saw thousands of tombstones. It suddenly dawned on me that some of them represented lives that spent a great deal of time on this planet.

Others represented lives that were only here for a very brief period of time. I began to see, with my spiritual eye, a wealth of aborted potential. There were doctors, lawyers, teachers, and Presidents who never blossomed into their full potential. The dreams and plans, hopes and purposes they were intended to obtain were now buried with them.

If we could talk to each of them, I am quite sure we would hear a long list of excuses why they never achieved their dreams. I felt as if I could hear them saying out loud, "I was poor and I didn't have any money. I was born in a third world country and I didn't have the opportunity people have in the west. I was not born into the right race."

I could go on and on with a list of reasons why this cemetery is rich with untapped potential and broken dreams, but the reality I came away with that day was that we have only a little time to accomplish our tasks on earth.

Everyone has reasons why he shouldn't realize his dreams. Even Paul said, *"I am the least of the apostles, that am not meet to be called an apostle, because I persecuted the church of God."* But Paul didn't stop there. He went on to say, *"But by the grace of God I am what I am: and His grace which was bestowed upon me was not in vain; but I laboured more abundantly than they all: yet not I, but the grace of God which was with me"* (1 Corinthians 15:9, 10).

I want to challenge you to write your own obituary right now. Think about it. What would it say? Would it echo the litany of accomplishments that you were able to fulfill, or would it read simply, 'Mr. Jones was a good man who left all his relatives behind?' I challenge you to think really hard about this and from today onward, start writing your obituary daily, in real time, and soon you will realize you are moving forward toward your goal.

There are others who have a great amount of natural skill and ability and believe they can get by solely on their talent.

Talent alone cannot take you to the place where you can maximize your gift and call. You have to have an undivided and passionate drive to stretch yourself and maintain focus on your prize, even in the midst of trials and tribulation. Maximizing your gift and call also means you have to be willing to swim in the deep water. So launch out, take risks, and go outside of your comfort zone.

Some of life's greatest success stories are born out of the greatest of failures. If you are afraid of failure and rejection, you will never maximize your talents and experience success. The ultimate result of true success is overcoming obstacles, disappointments and setbacks.

You may be thinking that there are circumstances beyond your control that are blocking your progress and keeping you from achieving the success you long for. Let me assure you that it is this kind of thinking that will keep you from your goal every time. The more negativity you allow to stay in your conversation and mind, the less you will have the fire and passion for achievement.

Please take note: God has granted you everything you need to succeed. With this in mind, look at your short comings as temporary setbacks and remember that failing does not make you a failure. You only become a failure when you fail to learn from what went wrong and make the necessary adjustments to bring forth positive change.

"Setbacks are set ups for come backs."

The key to maximizing your talent is to persevere through the most challenging and difficult times in your life. God knew that we would face obstacles and challenges and even fall short from time to time. He knew this so well that the entire plan of salvation was designed to address the failures and the shortcomings of mankind.

Through the work at Calvary, we have the power to maximize our gifts. If, however, we do not apply that finished work to our lives, it will never take root and grow. And many of us do not access this inherent power because of fear.

Fear is a factor in the lack of development and progress in our lives. I have seen so many talented people who were never able to realize their dream because they had such a strong fear of failure. They lacked the faith to believe that God had given them all that they needed to succeed.

There are some who say, "If I had what brother or sister so-and-so had, I would be successful." That, my friend, is an insult to the very God who created the one and only, unique, you! I know it sounds absolutely unthinkable, but there are people who suffer from the fear of success. I have seen them fail to even attempt to reach their maximum potential because of the fear of accountability and responsibility that comes with that level of success.

Then there are others who do not reach the maximum output of their talent because they are simply satisfied with their present state and don't see a need to progress. As a result of this, there is great amount of potential lost among many of our creative individuals. These human treasures are trapped and many have been aborted. Most people live in minimum performance mode, just doing enough to get by and not pushing themselves to greater limits. They are satisfied with a 'status quo' mentality. They do only what is required and expected. But there is a great testimony to be revealed if we can lose all of our negative, self-imposed limitations and launch out.

You may be sitting there reading this book and saying to yourself, "Mel, I want to launch out but I have somehow become jaded by the poison of popular opinion." Taking the plunge is never easy, but the final reward is definitely worth the jump. You never drown by jumping in the water, you drown when you fail to swim. When we make this plunge, we are denying ourselves of present pleasure for future reward.

I want to encourage you to read and study the Word of God, daily. A very good practice is to read a Proverb in the morning for instruction and read a Psalm at night for reflection. In the pages of God's word you will find every key to success that there is. There are so many examples of people who stood against the odds and won a victorious battle. If we follow every example set before us by the Lamb of God, we will see a clear pattern for success. Remember, there is no failure in Christ!

I have heard people say, "Jesus had an advantage. He was the Son of God!" When Christ came to this earth He laid aside His deity and sovereign power and became as any other man. He *"was in all points tempted like as we are, yet without sin"* (Hebrews 4:15).

He could have chosen a different path, another ending, or another life altogether, but He didn't. He chose to become a man and live like a man so He could show all of us how to live an overcoming life. The next time you feel as if you want to find out how to achieve the greatest levels of success, read the Word of God!

Remember this, my friend, Jesus made choices and decisions that led Him on a path of total success. You too can be on that path to living a successful Christian life if you make the right decisions today. Joshua said, *"choose you this day whom ye will serve"* (Joshua 24:15). I say; you will never regret choosing Christ!

Fast Forward:

†

What are you currently doing to maximize your talent?

†

What obstacles or challenges have you encountered along the way?

NOTES

CHAPTER TWENTY-FOUR
~MINISTRY~

When you hear someone mention the word 'ministry', what comes to mind? If you live in Great Britain, you might be reminded of the Prime Minister and the different facets of government. If you are in Israel, your first thought could be the Minister of Foreign Affairs. For a great many years the title 'reverend' was a sure give away that someone was in ministry. No matter if you think of a rabbi, priest, missionary, evangelist, pastor, apostle, prophet or minstrel, the word 'ministry' will apply to all of them, because ministry is all about people sharing the most precious gift ever created.

Ministry in its purest form is caring about someone's soul to the point that you will tell him that God so loved the world that He gave His only begotten son, Jesus Christ, to die for that person's sins. This can be shared in many ways; as creative artists we have the ability to use our creativity to present this message, which is the essence of ministry.

Too many have the misconception that ministry is based on what instead of who. We may even think performances, recordings, or books written are all done for the glory of God. I am sorry to tell you but that is just not the case. The truth is that every week there are thousands of media-related items being released into the marketplace that just happen to be non-secular, faith-based works. Many creative artists who produce these products, have a heart for God and ministry, but the question remains, what is the motive behind their actions?

God does not need another media-related product to promote His agenda. What God needs and wants is people with a servant's heart who have surrendered their lives to Him. The elements required for a balanced ministry can be found in two words, relationship and fellowship. Our relationship is anchored in our spirit and our soul is anchored in our fellowship. Our ministry will not be pure if either of these is not centered and balanced.

> *"They that worship Him must worship Him in spirit and in truth."*
> **John 4:24**

Personally, I define ministry as unconditional giving. To give on this level, one's relationship with God must be current, vibrant and passionate. It is important to have a relationship with God. The quality of our ministry is based solely on our fellowship with God, which in turn will create a relationship rich in the gifts of God. Our fellowship is measured by the quality time we spend with God in prayer and in His Word.

We should all have seasons and times of celebration, worship, studying the Word, repentance, forgiveness, restoration, and reconciliation. These are the things that should matter to you and me, because they matter to God. God sees how we live our lives both publicly and privately. It is not enough just to walk up on the stage at the Grammy's and other award shows to accept an award and thank God. It seems that a nod to God has become the politically correct thing to do. God deserves more than the superficial nod some offer Him. The only person that kind of action impresses can be found sitting in the audience or watching the show on television.

If you have an opportunity to produce various types of media-related projects, remember they should be done with the understanding that they are basically tools. They should never be the focal point of the ministry. These tools can be a tremendous blessing to you and the body of Christ, but they have no eternal benefit to God. God looks to you to present your body as a holy and acceptable offering to Him, that is the best way to represent God in ministry.

> *"I beseech you therefore, brethren, by the mercies of God, that ye present your bodies a living sacrifice, holy, acceptable unto God, which is your reasonable service. And be not conformed to this world: but be ye transformed by the renewing of your mind, that ye may prove what is that good, and acceptable, and perfect, will of God."* Romans 12:1, 2

All our innovative ideas have no real value to God if our lives are not pleasing to Him. God does not want us to conform to the patterns and structure of this society, but instead be transformed by the renewing of our minds with godly principles. Once this is accomplished, His approval is given and our ministry becomes very effective.

> *"When we walk in God's perfect will
> it transforms our ministry as a act of worship,
> it's our worship that gets God excited."*

Could it be that we have become far too dependent on others to lead us into the presence of God? Have we come to the place where we must have external assistance to help us worship God? Everyone has the ability to enter into the presence of God, no matter what your talent or musical ability might be.

Whether you play a tambourine or the tuba, you can create an inviting atmosphere for God to inhabit. This comes through what we do in our personal times of devotion. We should have a time set aside in our practice routine where we minister to God through worship, then hearing from God and playing unto the Lord. It is during this time of offering our talents back to God that He releases creativity, which in turn produces a higher level of skill and ultimately His anointing on our lives.

Just use the tools God has given you. God wants us to encourage one another with *"psalms, hymns, and spiritual songs"* (Ephesians 5:19). Remember, worship is birthed out of your spirit and not your talent. Fellowship with God creates relationship. Relationship evokes adoration. When we worship, we are saying that being in the presence of

God is where we find eternal value because He is truly worthy of adoration.

David was the chief musician in the temple. Part of his ministry was to train the musicians to live a lifestyle of worship. As a shepherd who played the lyre, a simple stringed instrument, he wrote and orchestrated music that proclaimed God in all of His majesty.

David's musical works were called psalms. That word comes from the Greek word 'psallo', which means, "to pluck a string." The book of Psalms was originally known as a book of songs for stringed instruments. David meticulously taught the Levitical priesthood order in the temple and the discipline of worship by using songs and musical instruments. This teaching made the temple musicians well versed in ushering the presence of God into the temple. Their understanding that worship is a verb presented three kinds of worship.

1. **LISTENING**
2. **SPEAKING**
3. **DOING**

Our ministry should be surrounded by a high level of worship among the contemporary Levitical order. The conscious realization of His presence in our houses of worship parallels what David taught in the temple. The warmth that comes with the feeling of knowing that He is in our midst, even without physically seeing Him, is what everyone needs to experience. God always desires that we seek Him, and in that earnest search, He reveals Himself to us because God's presence is everywhere. God is omnipresent.

"Draw near to God and He will draw near to you."
James 4:8 NKJV

We enter into God's presence by preparing our hearts. In order for us to have His presence in our midst, we must take two very important steps in our relationship with Him.

FIRST STEP: FORGIVENESS

As we draw near to the Lord, immediately the Holy Spirit reveals any sin that is in us. Confession and repentance of our sins prepares us to enter into God's presence. Once we confess our sins to the Lord and accept His loving mercy and forgiveness, we are restored.

"Repent therefore and be converted, that your sins may be blotted out, so that times of refreshing may come from the presence of the Lord."
Acts 3:19 NKJV

The word 'refreshing' means recovery of breath or revival. True revival begins with repentance and then we become renewed and restored by the Holy Spirit, the 'Breath of Life'.

"Create in me a clean heart, O God, and renew a steadfast spirit within me. Do not cast me away from your presence, and do not take Your Holy Spirit from me. Restore to me the joy of your salvation, and uphold me by your generous Spirit."
Psalms 51:10-12 NKJV

SECOND STEP: THANKSGIVING

After we have asked for forgiveness of our sins, we have prepared the way for Christ to act on our behalf. It's through salvation that Jesus Christ gives us the right to enter into God's presence. Now that we have re-established our communion with God we can bring an offering of thanksgiving, praise, and worship.

> *"Serve the LORD with gladness; Come before His presence with singing. Know that the LORD, He is God; It is He who has made us, and not we ourselves; We are His people and the sheep of His pasture. Enter into His gates with thanksgiving, And into His courts with praise. Be thankful to Him, and bless His name. For the LORD is good; His mercy is everlasting, and His truth endures to all generations."*
> Psalms 100:2-5 NKJV

I want to encourage you to take those two steps, forgiveness and thanksgiving, if you find your relationship and fellowship with God is not what it should be. There is nothing like being in the presence of God. Likewise, there is no greater thrill than to see a congregation truly worshipping the Lord with their whole body, soul and spirit. If you are called to lead people into worship, make certain your ministry to Him happens long before you arrive on the platform to lead worship. Our garments as priests should be spotless and without wrinkle. We must ensure that our ministry to Him and for Him is pure, undefiled and always giving God the praise, adoration and glory.

Fast Forward:

†

What can you do to increase the value of your ministry to God?

†

What are some of the fruits of your ministry?

NOTES

NOTES

CHAPTER TWENTY-FIVE
~FELLOWSHIP~

Your talents, skills and abilities may impress the world, but God is not impressed or moved by your great performances. God is more interested in the quality of your fellowship with Him. Remember, it's not your skills, talents, abilities or even your relationship that moves God, it's your fellowship. Why? The answer is because you can't have a relationship without fellowship.

Your fellowship with God is determined by the quality time you set aside to spend with God in prayer and in His Word.

Once a mother gives birth, the relationship of mother and child is established. If that mother never spends time with that newborn baby, their fellowship will never be established even though there is a legal relationship. Fellowship is the next level in a relationship. As you add depth to your fellowship with God, through the Word of God you will experience the change needed to create spiritual growth.

The effectiveness of our talents will also increase as we add depth to our fellowship. As artists we have to truly balance our time effectively. It is not always about how great we can be or how we develop our talent. It is even more important that we develop and constantly add depth to our fellowship with God the Father. When we view God as Father, this gives sight to a nuturing communion. The steps to obtaining this are spending time in prayer and studying His Word.

Paul, the apostle, said that you should *"Study to shew thyself approved unto God, a workman that needeth not to be ashamed, rightly dividing the word of truth"* (2 Timothy 2:15). God's symbols of approval are miracles, signs, and wonders. (See Mark 16:15-18) Jesus was *"a man approved of God...by miracles and wonders and signs, which God did by him"* (Acts 2:22). Fellowship with the Father was the source of Jesus' power. *"God anointed Jesus of Nazareth with the Holy Ghost and with power: who went about doing good, and healing all that were oppressed of the devil; for God was with him"* (Acts 10:38).

Fellowship is the source of our power. Being a bold witness is how God expects us to use that power. *"But ye shall receive power, after that the Holy Ghost is come upon you: and ye shall be witnesses unto me both in Jerusalem, and in all Judaea, and in Samaria, and unto the uttermost part of the earth"* (Acts 1:8).

When you are constantly talking about God, that conversation renews your faith and sharpens your knowledge of Him. You can share your faith through your creative talents by simply applying the Word of God to your life. This can be demonstrated through daily situations where you make choices and decisions that bring glory to God and honor Him.

Some time ago I was asked to play for a prominent Christian church event as a member of the horn section. I discerned somewhere in the midst of the event that one of the other musicians in the horn section was annoyed about something. Suddenly he expressed his discontent in a very secular manner. As a matter of fact, the way he responded was down-right rude! Many questions went through my mind as I observed this behavior. I could not understand why a church of this caliber would hire someone who was not a Christian and lacked basic respect for Christian principles.

He was very critical about the other musicians in the horn section and made very negative remarks about everyone. I was truly upset and my natural man began to rise. Suddenly I heard God whisper in my ear and said, 'The natural man does not understand the things of the spirit and he is only acting out of his natural nature. It's up to you who are in fellowship with me to bring forth the things of the Spirit."

I held my peace and started to pray. When he realized that he did not have a sparring partner, he backed down. After the service I shook his hand and told him I enjoyed playing with him and wished him well. You should have seen the look on his face. He thought I was going to deal with him in the same manner he had wanted to deal with me.

We are all faced with uncomfortable situations at times and, to be totally honest, we do not always handle them as we should. The real discrepancy is that we are new creations in Christ Jesus and therefore should act like it instead of opting to return momentarily to our old Adamic nature. We do not honor God or bring glory to Him when we choose to react instead of choosing to inspire and lead by example.

Remember, as your fellowship grows deep so does your character and integrity. As creative artists we occupy the stage so often; as a result of that we are held to a higher standard, and only through our fellowship with God can we maintain this standard. When others see the results of talent by virtue of our fellowship with God, they too will desire to change their lives.

Fast Forward:

†

What are you doing consistently to increase your fellowship with God?

†

Can you demonstrate your fellowship with God through your talent?

NOTES

NOTES

CHAPTER TWENTY-SIX
~SEED~

I like the parable of the talents because it presents a very realistic illustration of skill, gifts, and ability being used, planted, or invested like a seed. This very popular parable, found in the twenty-fifth chapter of the gospel according to Matthew, uses the literal use of the word 'talent' – a man's worth measured in gold.

When we put our talents to use in the kingdom of God, it is our service to God. We have no value to God if we are idle and don't invest - sow - the seed He has given us stewardship over. Like any responsible investor, God expects to make a profit. He wants a return on His investment. No matter how great or small you may perceive your talent or seed to be, it was imparted to you by God and His good favor, for a divine purpose.

> *"Every seed has a wealth of potential, opportunity and promise in it."*

God has given you talent to use and develop. In fact, everything we possess is from God. We have nothing we can call our own but our sin. He gave talent to you so you would have a starting point to exercise your faith and giving.

> *"For as the rain cometh down, and the snow from heaven, and returneth not thither, but watereth the earth, and maketh it bring forth and bud, that it may give seed to the sower, and bread to the eater: So shall my word be that goeth forth out of my mouth: it shall not return unto me void, but it shall accomplish that which I please, and it shall prosper in the thing whereto I sent it"* (Isaiah 55:10,11).

If your seed does not move your faith, it does not move God. It is our faith that excites God and brings results. So, it is first a walk by faith that moves us to invest our talent, which allows our talent to grow and develop. Any smart farmer looks for the most fertile ground in which to deposit his seed because he knows fertile ground will give his seed the best chance to grow to its highest potential. Our seed has the ability to produce something much greater than itself, provided it is placed in a fertile environment.

> *"Verily, verily, I say unto you, Except a kernel of wheat fall into the ground and die, it abideth alone: but if it die, it bringeth forth much fruit"* (John 12:24).

The Bible teaches that seeds have the ability to reproduce *"after his kind"* (Genesis 1:11). In every illustration, however, the success of the seed is determined by what the sower did with the seed. You see the seed - our talent - is what we plant. Planting displays our faith and expectation, and that is what moves God and brings forth the harvest.

I have seen many talented and creative individuals who have never reached their potential because they aborted their seed. Please take note that the plan of Satan in the redemption process is always to destroy the seed. So Satan wants so dearly to stop every opportunity for a seed to develop into that great structure which God intended it to be. There is nothing sadder than to watch a truly talented person begin to use his talent for God, then over time, it fades because of secular distractions.

The secular path has become crowded with hundreds of thousands of people trying to be the next superstar. Losing the revelation that Christ is the only superstar has taken its toll. God never intended to give you a talent solely to satisfy yourself. He gave you talent so the world could see His glory through you; as you enjoy it and use it, He is glorified.

> *"For all things are for your sakes,
> that the abundant grace might through the thanksgiving of
> many redound to the glory of God."*
> **2 Corinthians 4:15**

Once again we arrive at the crossroads of relationship. Either you have a relationship with God or you don't. Our actions reveal who the real master of our life is.

God never gives you a seed that you do not need. In fact, many times we fall short in our realization that what He has given us is something that is necessary to fulfill our purpose. A seed cannot reproduce unless it is sown. It is God's goal for you to develop and grow and to see His investment in you bring bountiful returns.

Please take note that development of your seed is not automatic and it is not a one-time event. The development of your seed is a process that takes time and must be joined with an intentional and deliberate commitment. You want to invest and sow because that is the only way the seed can grow. God is not going to sow your seed for you. Failure to sow your seed will result in spiritual abortion and here are a few ways that can happen.

- **Failure to spend time in God's Word.**
- **Failure to spend time in prayer.**
- **Failure to consistently attend worship services.**
- **Failure to spend time developing your talent.**

Your seed has life and will always produce after its kind. When we observe a seed in its natural state, our physical senses are incapable of judging whether a seed is alive or dead. No one can see, feel, hear, smell, or taste the life in a seed. There is only one way to prove a seed is alive. Sow it! Here are some ways seeds are sown.

- **Planting the Word of God in your heart and mind.**
- **Giving of your time and talent in service to others.**
- **Giving of your tithes and offerings.**
- **Frequent attendance at worship services.**

God will lead you to places where there is fertile soil to sow your seed. This may be an organization or someone who has a proven track record in stewardship and handling the things of God. The best way to plant the seed of God's Word in your life is by speaking the Word. Hearing others speak the Word is good, but that will not produce as bountiful a harvest as when you are speaking the Word yourself.

When Saul was anointed king of Israel, the prophet Samuel told him that he would meet a company of prophets coming down the hill of God playing instruments and prophesying. He told Saul that the spirit of God would come upon him and that when he prophesied with them, he would be turned into *"another man"* (1 Samuel 10:1-6).

Speaking God's word with your mouth is essential. As we speak God's word, we are planting the seed in our heart for the harvest we desire.

"For with the heart one believes to righteousness, and with the mouth confession is made to salvation."
Romans 10:10

Whatever you need to be saved or delivered from, confession (what you say) is essential. If you sense in your heart that you need to affirm and confess that God's word will produce exactly what it is supposed to, then I invite you to make the following declaration, out loud, right where you are.

SAY THESE WORDS...

God's Word is a seed that will produce blessing in my life, so I will plant it in my heart and mind by hearing it, reading it, and speaking it.

Intentions can be hidden but our actions are obvious. Make certain that your intentions and your actions reside at the same address so that absolute clarity is achieved! One out of alignment with the other can be so misleading. It also can cause you great confusion as to the direction you want to go. Remember, the double-minded man is *"unstable in all his ways,"* and should not expect to *"receive any thing of the Lord"* (James 1:6-8).

If your heart is divided, you can never give your heart totally to God. You must have a single purpose in place before you can rest assured that God is going to allow the explosion of expression – the harvest from your seed, your talent, sown -- that you so desire to happen in your life and talent.

Fast Forward:
†
What are you doing to fertilize your seed?
†
Where has God placed you to plant your seed?

NOTES

NOTES

CHAPTER TWENTY-SEVEN
~MATURITY~

A mature individual is someone who does not think only in absolutes, is able to be objective even when deeply stirred emotionally, has learned that there is both good and bad in all people and all things and walks humbly and deals charitably.

What are the marks of maturity? It's not solely the result of time or longevity. The basic grassroots meaning of maturity is learning how to walk in obedience to God. Maturity is a process that requires time in order for it to manifest. You may be born with a specific talent but it will take time for that talent to mature. For some the time frame may be short, but at the end of the day it all boils down to your willingness to accept the responsibility of developing your talent. There are several key components that aid in the process of becoming mature, so you may want to take a pen and underscore them as I mention them.

These key components are the building blocks of Godly character. The first and foremost component is responsibility, which provides the necessary foundation for your creativity to expand and become a powerful force. Over time responsibility will steadily build your creative credibility. Credibility is also a key component in the maturation process. There are four major components we need to adhere to if we are truly going to mature. These are vitally important, especially to the creative community. These components may seem easy for the most part, but in reality are difficult to master.

Recognize that obtaining maturity means practicing self-discipline. The first victory we must win is self-control. You can use many different ways to activate this. However, the desire to control your flesh and make sound ethical and moral decisions is paramount to your successfully achieving a mature life. I cannot stress enough the need for you to be careful not to make decisions that bring you temporary gratification while clearly mortgaging your future.

One highly successful business executive, John Weston, stated it this way. "I have always tried to live my life with a simple rule: Don't do anything that you would not feel comfortable reading about in the newspaper the next day." Every time you make a strong decision to do the right thing, you are strengthening your self-discipline, thus excelling in maturity.

Complete what you start. People who are truly mature follow through and follow up. In our churches today we are truly talent rich, but in so many cases the results are less than stellar. The reason is that so many talented people lack commitment. Let me give you an example. Take a minute right now and write your obituary. Now that you have done that task, or at least given it some deep thought, let me ask you a simple question. If you were honest when writing your obituary, is it a true representation of your life up to this point? Does it clearly state all the things you have positively completed? We all prefer not to think about death, and the good news here is if you are reading this chapter you are not dead! That means you still have time to use the power to complete what you have started.

Be Dependable. Talent never succeeds on its own. You mature through a sequence of events, which are usually birthed out of a myriad of relationships. In these relationships you will find circumstances where you will have to depend on others, and there will be times when others will need to depend on you. That codependent act is truly what teamwork is all about. Remember, having intentions to do something is commendable, but the true result of maturity is being dependable by turning your intentions into action.

Accept Responsibility. Don't expect others to step in and do what you are not willing to do for yourself. God will send people into your life to help and assist you along the way, but never get to the point where you become lazy and totally rely on them to get the work done. Mature individuals take action at the appropriate time and know when to be still. Be responsible even in your mistakes. Most people who truly made a difference decided to do their best and not give up.

These key components will always be found on the road to maturity. Learning from each one of these key components will ensure that your talent is seasoned with just the right amount of balance. How many of us would be on the fast track to maturity if we were rewarded a million dollars every time we made an accomplishment. Maybe that reference is a bit extreme, but all too often we are motivated by things rather than by correct choice.

As you develop in your maturation process, you may go through what seems to be a series of never ending seasons of preparation, then suddenly you are promoted and God sets the stage right in the middle of everything and everyone around you. When God declares a new season in your life, you suddenly have the potential of reaching your dream, so don't miss out and waste it. If you let anything redirect your path, you may find yourself back in the preparation stage season! God never intended for you to go from glory back to preparation. His plan is for us to go from glory to glory!

As stated earlier the components that lead to maturity are not easy to master because we all face struggles in these houses of flesh that are often tempted and must be constantly disciplined. You will always feel the persistent pull of Satan trying to get you to do something immoral. Satan does not mind that you are saved. He couldn't care less about your relationship with God. What he is interested in is making sure you never mature into your purpose in God.

If Satan can keep you circling in the wilderness where there is nothing but discouragement and lack of direction that will eventually crush the desire to seek out your promised land, then he is content. That is something you and I cannot afford to have happen. We must not camp in the desert of misdirected plans. We must never stop moving toward the horizon of purpose. The minute you begin operating in your purpose and fulfilling your assignment, Satan knows that you can become a threat unless you are sidetracked. That is why Satan seeks to keep us idle and doing nothing or busy and distracted with insignificant stuff. He will use the simplest of things such as people, places and the most ridiculous issues imaginable just to keep us from growth and maturity.

Some time ago I was employed as the bandleader with a Pilgrim Church in Brooklyn, New York. It is a very effective and prominent ministry. I loved my job and was very happy to serve God in this capacity. My responsibilities were to arrange the music and manage the musicians in the band. I was always on time and worked many more hours than were required. I was in every sense of the word 'faithful'.

One Friday in June I was doing the weekly radio broadcast. When the time came for the countdown for the band to begin playing, I was asked to sit down and not proceed. I was surprised to say the least. I wondered what in the world was going on when suddenly the word came from the pulpit that the entire band was released from their services. In other words, we were FIRED!

To this day we still are unclear as to the purpose of this action. I couldn't believe what I was hearing. I was devastated. I thought, "How wrong is this, especially when I am giving my best effort to do my job to the best of my ability?" Something burned inside me. I became very bitter and commented that I was not going to be employed by a church ever again. That was exactly what the enemy wanted me to do.

God will allow circumstances to push you toward your next assignment. The key is to trust Him!

What I did not realize then was that God had His hand on the entire situation though it was painful. Events were working together for my good. For a brief moment I forgot *"that all things work together for good to them that love God, to them who are the called according to his purpose."* (Romans 8:28) I had grown comfortable in that position and God knew He had to allow this situation to get my attention so I could truly mature. What the enemy was trying to do was stagnate me. He wanted me to stay mad at the Pastor and blame him. If he could win that single battle, he could get me to operate outside of God's purpose for my life. Once I understood what was happening, I had to make the tough decision to walk in God's love. This in and of itself is the essence of maturity.

As creative beings we are constantly being presented with circumstances where we have to make tough decisions. Our level of maturity will guide us through this process. In the midst of these decisions we will find the circumstances we encounter may last for a season while at the same time revealing God's distinct purpose. The good news is that these decisions get easier when love is the cornerstone of your character. Being like Christ means you love like Him and forgive like Him. He also proved that a young man of thirty-three can have immense wisdom and maturity if he will stay centered on being about His Father's business.

Remember, the Word of God teaches that we are to love one another, forgive one another and restore one another. The true test of our maturity is to live what the Word of God teaches and allow it to become who we are. This takes work and practice and often times it can be an arduous task. The exciting news is we have the power to be victorious and truly live a life as mature children of God!!

Fast Forward:
†
What are doing in your ministry
that will help you to mature?
†
How many of the four components discussed in this
chapter are you applying to your life?

NOTES

CHAPTER TWENTY-EIGHT
~BATTLES~

On our pursuit of our creative call we will all come to a point where we will be faced with some kind of obstacle. In some cases these obstacles may be battles. Whether they are spiritual or physical, we are going to have to get through them. Your victory lies in your faith and your ability to use the information God has given to you.

There are laws that regulate the flow of all kinds of commercial information. The terms 'input' and 'output' refer to the processing and communication between incoming and outgoing data of a dedicated system. "I/O" is a very popular term in the computer processing world that defines this process. Most people have a computer which has an operating system on board. The "Central Processing Unit," better known as the CPU, is the brain of the computer and is where most calculations take place. In computer language, the CPU is the principal element of a computer system and is crucial to its operation.

In a spiritual context, input is the data which is placed into you by God, such as a talent. Everything that goes in (Input) will be processed (CPU) in the CPU where we have the majority of our battles, because there are spiritual forces that want the output to be ineffective. God has placed gifts and talents into every one of us. Some of these gifts are identifiable at a very young age and others may take us a lifetime to discover. So, whether you find out what your gift or talent is at three or ninety-three, you still need to activate it.

No matter how large or small you perceive your talent to be, it requires attention, time, study, and polishing with the gentle touch of love that will make it shine. Sometimes people or material things have to be removed because of how they are attached, but once this is lovingly done, we discover that it was for our own good. Once we discover that precious gift of talent, which was deposited in our life, we must maintain it.

Yes, there is even a battle that is faced when we begin to maintain the treasure we have in earthen vessels. Maintenance is always much more of a challenge because it is easier to obtain than to maintain. That gift or talent that God gave you was the easiest thing in the world for you to receive. You didn't have to fight for it; you didn't have to save for years to accumulate the funds to buy it. You didn't have to place it on a credit card and go into debt to pay for it. It was a good, wholesome gift with no strings attached. All you were required to do was to be responsible for the stewardship over it.

> *"Every good and perfect gift is from above,*
> *Coming down from the Father of the heavenly lights,*
> *Who does not change like shifting shadows."*
> James 1:17 NIV

You must realize that Satan, the enemy of your soul, is distraught and extremely jealous of what God gave you. He literally wants to steal it from you. Remember, he once held the ultimate creative position in the kingdom of Heaven. He was an awesome musician and singer; he was even more talented than Michael Jackson, Steve Wonder and Liberace all rolled into one.

And guess what? He lost it all! Every bit of it! Now here man comes along and God bestows the most treasured gifts of creativity in him. Not only is Satan upset that you have been given what he used to have, he wants to totally obliterate what God has given you. He doesn't even care if you become collateral damage in the process. All that matters is that you don't get to enjoy the full benefits of that gift!

The driving force behind Satan's jealous hatred is his knowledge that he has lost the Love of the Lord. He was once the star of the morning and now must bow his knee to the Bright and Morning Star, Jesus Christ. Everywhere he looks he sees the love of God bestowed upon man. He sees the gifts God has given you! He hates you for it and will do anything he can to make certain you never mature in that gift. He will use every trick in the book to lure you away from your destiny in God.

He will use fame, fortune, friends, family and every weakness you possess to thwart the plan of God. Satan's jealousy slays love under the pretense of nurturing it. This is why we must gain wisdom in our walk with Christ. It is true that love has a sharp eye; it sees sharply while hatred sees even more so. King Solomon discovered the wiles of jealousy and revealed that jealousy was as unyielding as the grave. We must guard our hearts and our minds in order to be able to maintain the inner workings of God's gift in us.

> *"Place me like a seal over your heart,*
> *like a seal on your arm; for love is as strong as death,*
> *its jealousy unyielding as the grave.*
> *It burns like blazing fire, like a mighty flame."*
> Song of Solomon 8:6

Maintenance means that you are preventing a problem before it actually occurs by putting in place dedicated mechanisms that will circumvent any hazardous situation. This is done by developing the practice of having regular time with God in prayer and in the Word of God, either in the mornings, afternoons or evenings whichever is most convenient to your schedule. Consistency is paramount to maintenance. Having a consistent time even if it is short is better than long meditation at irregular times.

If you can make time to eat, check your email and go to the gym, you can make time to fellowship with your heavenly Father. Find a Bible-believing church and be committed to it spiritually, physically and financially. Have an accountability relationship with a pastor, mentor or teacher; this will help you to stay on track and you will experience victory in your battles.

> *Your destiny is connected to the relationships*
> *You maintain in your life.*

*You will either affect or be affected
by the company you keep.*

Fast Forward:
†
What battles are you currently fighting?
†
What have you learned during battle?

NOTES

CHAPTER TWENTY-NINE
~MODERATION~

*"For our struggle is not against flesh and blood,
but against the rulers, the authorities and the powers
of this dark world and against the spiritual forces of evil
in the heavenly realms."*
Ephesians 6:12

Many times on our creative journey we will experience an event or situations that may really shock us and even throw us for a loop. As it was for me, getting fired from the position I held at my then current church. Although at the time when that happened I was truly bruised and bitter, I eventually realized the firing was all part of God's plan and it was only a transitional period.

Before long I got my next assignment. Looking back at that situation and a few others I have encountered through the years, I realize I have learned a few insightful truths – truths I think you might find useful.

1. Moderation is the best way to go about anything. When you become excessive concerning anything you are engaged in, there is a tendency toward error.

2. Errors are much like the small splinters that stick you but you cannot see them, even though you can feel their effect. The reason for the splinter is we did not prepare the surface because we were in too much of a hurry.

3. Haste makes waste. I know the phrase is trite, but in this case, it's true. *"For which of you, intending to build a tower, sitteth not down first, and counteth the cost, whether he have sufficient to finish it? Lest haply, after he hath laid the foundation, and is not able to finish it, all that behold it begin to mock him, Saying, This man began to build, and was not able to finish"* (Luke 14:28-30). Time spent in preparation is never wasted time.

There is a little thing I call the principle of perverted perception. Don't ever allow your assignment to be greater than God! When you get so deep into your assignment that you forget to check in with the One who sent you -- you are in deep trouble. It is so easy to get caught up in what you are doing. Our misplaced sense of self-importance is birthed out of the demand for our talents, making it, all too often, difficult to remember we are on His assignment, not one of our own.

The demands of our church or employer hover over us, weighing on us. That is how we make our living. If we're not careful, we lose sight of the fact that God is in control. The pressure of the work can deceive us into thinking that we are indispensable, when in reality no one is. Add to that deception the additional stress that comes with a growing ministry, a blossoming music department and a few personal accolades and soon you will find that your eyes are no longer on God but staring in the mirror, not recognizing the face looking back at you. Let this psalm of David be your prayer.

> *"I will praise thee;*
> *for I am fearfully and wonderfully made:*
> *marvellous are thy works;*
> *and that my soul knoweth right well."*
> Psalm 139:14

O.K.! Let's make sure you have three very important lessons etched into your mind. Believe me, they will help you through trying times. Winning the battle begins with learning that God has already won it for you. Learning to praise Him for the victory will keep your mind balanced.

1. Anything done in excess leads to error.
2. Don't allow your assignment to be greater than God.
3. Keep your eyes on God while doing your assignment.

There is no doubt that God allowed me to get fired for my growth. He will allow similar things to happen to you. So don't be surprised when they do. Peter warned us when he wrote,

"Beloved, think it not strange concerning the fiery trial which is to try you, as though some strange thing happened unto you" (1 Peter 4:12).

The Law of Maturity is very simple: Time plus Process equals Growth. Over a period of time the process will do exactly what it has been designed to do. The process will present you before the Lord as a willing and humble servant, so that He can say, "Well done!"

I cannot close this chapter without addressing those who think that living in isolation from the Body of Christ is better than engaging with it. You may be staying away from the church because someone hurt you, disappointed you, or took advantage of you. But when you let the enemy put you on the shelf, you give him his victory. All you will do is grow more and more distant and possibly become hard-hearted and bitter.

The root of bitterness will create nothing but remorse and sorrow and in some cases sickness and even death. There is no benefit in isolation. Your growth can only be stimulated in a community environment where there is constant interaction.

"Let us draw near with a true heart in full assurance of faith, having our hearts sprinkled from an evil conscience, and our bodies washed with pure water. Let us hold fast the profession of our faith without wavering; (for he is faithful that promised;) And let us consider one another to provoke unto love and to good works: Not forsaking the assembling of ourselves together, as the manner of some is; but exhorting one another: and so much the more, as ye

see the day approaching" (Hebrews 10:22-25).

Jesus is coming soon. It would be a shame if you find yourself doing for God and your life is not anchored in God. If you can relate to this get back into the presence of the Lord. Let Him heal you and restore you. Remember balance is the key of life, which makes moderation possible.

Fast Forward:
†
Is there something currently on your plate
that is very time consuming?
†
What do you spend the most time doing daily?

NOTES

CHAPTER THIRTY
~USAGE~

"You can have the pattern without the Glory of God, but you cannot have the Glory of God without the pattern!"

Everything that God gives to us has a purpose. If we do not know the purpose of what we have, there is a chance that we might end up defeating the purpose and plan God has intended for us to excel in. To say that there are pitfalls in life is an understatement. We all struggle with adapting to any plan that we did not create in and of ourselves. When God introduces His purpose into our lives, there is a plan that comes with it, whose outcome is success. So, how do we ensure that we are following the purpose and plan of God? I'm glad you asked.

There are people who might say to you that it is impossible to know what God actually wants you to do. Let me ask you this question. Do you believe God speaks to people today? He spoke to kings, priests, prophets, shepherds, apostles in the Word of God and He has not changed the way He deals with man since. He still speaks to people today. The real issue here is whether we are listening and recognize His voice when He does speak. I cannot place enough importance on the need for intimacy with God. The more time you spend with Him and His Word the more likely you will be able to recognize His voice.

Taking the time to seek God in order to clearly understand the purpose the talents He has given you stewardship over is just part of the equation. Once you have this knowledge, it's time to engage your talent in order for the presence of God to flow through you.

People will sense the unction and anointing even as you are experiencing it, but in many different ways. Some will experience overwhelming love in action and unconditional compassion in the manifested presence of the Holy Spirit. And all of this can and will occur when our talents and gifts are centered in His plan and purpose.

There are countless ways to share your talent. You can perform a musical rendition or you can give words of comfort and encouragement. Either will present the environment for God's presence to be manifested. No matter how you choose to use your talent, use it!

It's not unusual that people struggle with the question as to how to use their gifts and talents, so let's find some common ground we can both stand on to discuss this topic. Let's agree you recognize you have a gift from God. Congratulations! This is a major hurtle you have just overcome. Being able to declare that you know you have a gift from God lets the devil know that you have made your mind up to follow His plan for your life. You are ready for the process of growing, learning and perfecting what is in you for His glory to begin. However, you may feel as if you are in the midst of indecision, so what do you do?

There are all kinds of questions that pop up at the first sign, upon the discovery that you have made a decision to serve in the Kingdom of God. You may wonder what part of the body of Christ you should be used in, or should you even be used in the body of Christ at all. That tiny little doubt is a key to knowing the direction you should take. This is a good time for you to take inventory of yourself and find out what is your motive and reason for wanting to do a certain task or use a certain gift or talent.

> *"The devil never inspires anyone to use*
> *his gifts and talents for God,*
> *and the Holy Spirit never inspires anyone…*
> *To use his gift to glorify the devil"*

God has a direct blue print for your life and it is essential to understand that plan. Oddly enough, the confusing part of this is that you will never know the complete plan for your life at any given time. You may be sitting there saying, "Great! Here I am, ready to go, and now you tell me to relax!" Remember that I told you in previous chapters about the process? Well, here we go! This is part of it. God reveals His purpose and plan to you in levels and stages.

If He showed you the big picture from start to finish, it would probably overwhelm you or scare you so badly that you would run from doing anything for God.

God has designed the process for our own good. If we knew the trials we would have to endure beforehand, many of us would just throw in the towel and quit. I know that if God had told me it was going to be seventeen years after I finished high school before my musical career was off the ground, I would have told Him there had to be a better way! If God would have told me that during that period of time I would be unemployed, a street musician, a vacuum cleaner salesman, cleaning toilets in the church and a chauffeur for the Pastor, I would have probably told God to "Hit the Road, Jack!"

What was first and foremost in all of those seasons was one single and very powerful word God placed in my spirit. He told me that He was going to make me the head and not the tail, and that I was more than a conqueror. At first I sincerely wondered if I had heard correctly. But, after time went by, I saw all of these promises come to pass, all in God's time.

God created time for man so he could measure the events and actions that transpired between him and his Creator. God does not operate on our human clock because time does not exist for Him. God's time is always now! One thing I have learned is that every one of these all-important events was needed in order to prepare me for my call and purpose.

So many Christians short-change the blessings that God has for them because they do not fully understand that God has provided not only talents but also gifts for the church. These gifts came through Jesus Christ in the form of the five-fold ministries. They were given in order that the saints would be perfected for the work of the ministry. Apostles, prophets, evangelists, pastors and teachers are gifts from God to the body of Christ, just as your gift and talent have been given to you in order to bless the Body of Christ.

When we fail to celebrate the presence of all these gifts in our lives, we lose the blessing that comes through them. If you do not receive a prophet, you cannot partake of his anointing. This same principle applies to every one of the five gifts. This same principle applies to a musician and a singer. If you do not receive their gift to the Lord, you will not benefit from it. One of the more misunderstood gifts is that of the pastor. Before you get twisted about this, let me reassure you that I am only bringing this to your attention because so many people lack insight as to how they are to view the man or woman of God in the role of pastor.

Your pastor is not your "home-boy" or hang-out buddy; when you place him in these positions you circumvent the anointing he has to speak wholeheartedly into your life. Also you can become too familiar and lose respect for his God delegated office. If you truly want to see the floodgates of Heaven burst wide open, reverence and honor your pastor. I encourage you to operate in this mindset and you will not be guilty of pastoral misuse. When we understand the purpose of our pastor, we will experience unity in our house of worship.

Unity is much like the protocol of the operating system on your CPU. If everything is in order, the programs run effortlessly. If there is something that is not in line with the protocol, the computer will crash. When unity is present, the gifts can flow unhindered and have their full effect. When unity is not there, the gifts may continue to operate but the overall effect is impacted by that invisible wall of opposition. I cannot imagine anyone wanting to go to a church where the unity is continually disrupted. Peace is a valuable treasure and when it is not present, our gifts and talents do not flourish in the manner they should.

Let me say it this way if you will allow me to, "You can have the pattern without the Glory of God, but you cannot have the Glory of God without the pattern!" God has a perfect plan and a wonderful process for you to experience. As long as you stay connected to God, He will always present you with a blueprint for you to use to ensure your success!

Fast Forward:
†
How are you using your talent currently?
†
How can you be more effective in the usage of your talent?

NOTES

NOTES

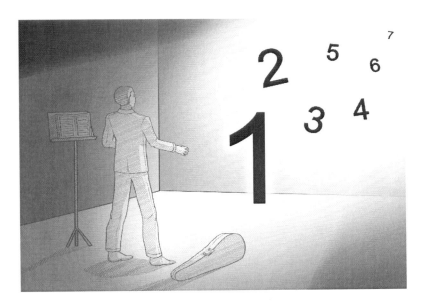

CHAPTER THIRTY-ONE
~PRIORITIES~

You will hear me say time and time again that I believe working for the richest Jew who ever walked the planet is quite a rewarding experience. Now let me clarify that statement by saying that the Jew I am referring to is Jesus Christ of Nazareth, the son of God, born into this world as a member of the Jewish faith. Being employed by Him is quite fulfilling and in the midst of this fulfillment I have to be very careful not to lose my focus and begin to pay more attention to the employment than I do God.

You see Satan does not mind you being busy in ministry as long as you are not effective. When we stretch ourselves to the place that our artistry is our biggest priority we have erred in our true service to God. Error is a seed which is germinated by Satan. Satan wants you to stay in ministry and operate in error because he knows that he then has a secret agent right in the middle of God's camp. Can you imagine being an emissary for the devil and not know it? That is exactly what happens when we lose focus!

Once you are involved in full time ministry it is very easy for creative artists to lose their way. You become so busy with rehearsals, recordings sessions, auditions and travel schedules that it becomes easy not to sequentially place things in a logical order. The neglect to prioritize the essentials will lead to a dysfunctional life. Whether we are married, in a relationship or single, God has outlined for us what our priorities should be and the order they should follow.

The bottom line is your ministry gift isn't about you!

Becoming so self-absorbed to the point of neglecting your friends, family and those you are ministering to makes you ineffective. The Order in which God has designed for you to live your life regardless of your status is something you must etch on your mind so that you will never forget how to approach life and the work of God.

1. God
2. Family
3. Career
4. Ministry
5. Yourself

Oh I can hear the groaning already! Oh well, too bad! This is God's Order, not mine. We have allowed the world to influence and corrupt our focus to the point where we think we are on the top of that list, not that anyone would admit it. For those who would never think of being so selfish, they think they are honoring God by putting their ministry first and this is just as wrong.

Let's delve a little deeper as to what this all means. God first should be self-explanatory. Where are you in your walk with the Lord? Do you have a specific time slot allotted for your devotions and prayer time? I am not talking about some kind of quickly spoken and rushed through prayer as you are heading out the door. This might be a good time to ask yourself; "Do I spend quiet time with the Lord just soaking in His presence and listening to Him speak to me? "When was the last time you fasted and prayed to get a clearer understanding of the magnitude of the call God has placed on your life and talent?

We all know we can find time to do what really matters to us. There is nothing that will stand in our way when we want to find hours to mindlessly sit in front of the TV or computer. There is nothing wrong with down time until it becomes all the time and keeps us from our family and God. I always found the term 'down-time' interesting. If we do prefer to spend time doing other things that are not exalting God, either in act or deed, then those fleshly things will eventually bring us down spiritually and eternally.

You should always have time to pray with your family! If not make the time! This seems to be the area that suffers the most as it is the desire of the enemy to destroy families. What better way to do it than under the guise of ministry? When this happens everyone blames God instead of the real culprit, Satan. When was the last time you had devotions with your spouse? I mean taking the time to read the Word, discuss the Word and praying the Word. Whether you are married or in a committed relationship, spending time with one another with God is essential to bringing balance and harmony in your lives.

God often uses your mate to confirm things, bring a word of encouragement or even direction that you may not see because you are too close to the matter. When we are in tune with one another, God can quicken our spiritual antenna on behalf of the person. When was the last time you spent quality time with your family, children included? Oh, I know some of you are saying; "Well, we all go to church together on Sunday and Wednesday and we have family game night on Friday."

That is all well and good, however, when was the last time you sat down to a meal with your family and you actually listened to them speak instead of the conversation turning into a discourse on you and your ministry? When was the last time you had family devotions and prayed for and with each of your children? When was the last time you anointed your children with oil and prayed for them? When was the last time you went out on a ministry date and you took your entire family, not so they could see what you do but more so they could see what God does when He ministers through you?

For many of us, our careers are ministry based and if this is true in your life you have an even tougher time keeping balance in this area. I want to address those who still work in the secular arena and minister on weekends. When you come to work on Monday morning, does your water cooler conversation sound like a 'who's who' and travelogue rolled into one?

Because truth be-told, your co-workers aren't as interested that you rubbed elbows with prophet so and so, or that you were the opening "act" for some Dove award winner. You are impressed with your own press which is a strong sign that you aren't secure in who and what God called you to. How much more pleasing to God would it be if when we entered the office and someone asked well how did your show go this weekend? You would say, "Well it wasn't a show I was ministering" in music, song, dance whatever.

You might find that your response will open a door for you to then share with them how God used you miraculously to minister to someone who was depressed or suicidal. Maybe someone was healed of cancer and that report is exactly what they needed to hear because someone in their family is going through that same sickness. When you shared that story, that is really what they want to hear as they have a void that needs to be filled and your testimony is just what they needed to hear.

Throughout this book we have been discussing your ministry and talent, so that is pretty clear by now. We will continue to discuss this element as the pages continue to turn, so stay tuned. As painful as it is to put oneself on the backburner so to speak, the Bible is clear about denying ourselves, keeping our focus on Him and dying daily to our humanity. It isn't easy, but it is a daily and sometimes hourly process, one that will strengthen our walk and ministry. Just remember the balanced view for your life; God, Family, Career, Ministry and Me!

Fast Forward:

†

What takes up the majority of your time daily?

†

What steps can you take to rearrange your priorities?

NOTES

NOTES

CHAPTER THIRTY-TWO
~ENVIRONMENT~

"There is nothing more important than creating an environment conducive to the flow of the Holy Spirit"

I cannot express enough to you the importance of this chapter. In fact, if I truly commented about the vast myriad of environmental issues we as artists face, this book would never reach its final page. The list is truly endless. With that in mind allow me to propose to you that we address the first of many key elements that surround this topic, personal space and time.

It is very important that you surround yourself with people who are going in the same direction as yourself. You can associate with everybody but you cannot hang out with everybody. Your time spent with people is paramount in shaping your future. An association is usually casual. Spending time with someone usually means a deeper depth of relationship. If you want to know something about someone, you can look at the people he spends most his time with.

We all have our personal time when we get away from the hustle and bustle of our work and the demands of life. Some people can hardly wait until it is Friday so they can lock their desk at work and lay the keys on the hall table until Monday morning so they can hit the street and meet friends and family for dinner and entertainment.

All of this is simply part of living our life as productive citizens on the planet. But there comes a time in all of this when everyone has said their goodbyes, gone home and left us to ourselves. If we are married we might find that there is a moment at the end of the day when private time arrives and each spouse finds a quiet place to reflect on his or her day.

All of these scenarios sound like the average American dream life, don't they? While they have that fuzzy warm feeling, there is a very important challenge that arrives in every one of these situations. When we are all alone, the challenge of producing an all-new environment arrives. We had our spouse, loved ones and friends around to help create the environment; now we are alone and must create a singular environmental setting.

It is in this private time where we are faced with the real us, the real person and not the artist or the creative talent. Suddenly we are inundated with one mental challenge after another until we either bow to the barrage of battering from the enemy or we rise above it and create the one and only safe environment for a child of God, worship.

I am not talking about church. I am talking about worship as a lifestyle. Instead of being led into sin and the lust of the flesh, the pride of life and the pursuit of power and prestige, we bow before God and give Him back our talents, abilities, time and space because we acknowledge they all came from Him in the first place. The fruit of our lips and the lyrics of our hearts are such that He can find joy in every moment we are alone with Him. Yes, I said that correctly, alone with Him. When you have nobody else around, who do you think is there? God!

The enemy would like to keep you from thinking about God, loving His Word and living large in His presence, but he knows the truth just as you and I do. Greater is He that is in us than He that is in the world. Our God is greater, more powerful, more wonderful and more exciting than anyone or anything that the kingdom of darkness can provide.

When you take the time to think about Him, talk to Him and sing to Him, you are creating an atmosphere filled with His glory. When we create glorious praise and worship, we are reproducing the original environment of Heaven. God can inhabit the praises of His people because Heaven's atmosphere is permeated with praise! God feels at home when our lifestyle is one of praise and worship.

Obedience to Him is the catalyst and divine determination is the solution that, when mixed together in thanksgiving, ..Produce peace.

No matter where you go, you can take His peace with you. If you will keep your mind stayed on Him, He will keep your mind in perfect peace. That peace that you carry around with you is actually something that people can sense and experience if you will live in it and not out of it. How many times have people said to you that they can sense something different about you but cannot quite figure it out? It is His presence in us that they feel. And it is eternally important that we do not open our mouths and destroy what God is doing through us.

The environment we create is affected by our words and actions. We must remember that we are His ambassadors and witnesses to this world, that He has risen from the dead and lives forever more, and that we now live and breathe and have our being in Christ! It is easy to be in a supernaturally charged environment in church, but what about taking that environment home with you and continuing in it while all alone?

I have learned that while I am ministering to the Body of Christ, I am pouring out of me what I have been filled with during my quiet times with Him. When I return home, I then can go to my secret place with Him and allow Him to restore my body, mind and spirit. All it takes is for me to create an environment for Him and He will be there, every time!

When you use your talents in ministry, they ascend to heaven as a fragrant offering to the Lord. Each word we speak in praise and worship to Him is received with love. Each song we sing to Him fills Him with joy which

He then returns to us in the form of strength. There is a tremendous power that is released when we begin to speak His name and declare His acts. That power changes the molecular structure of the atmosphere and charges it with His glory. It is essential that we walk in unity with one another and center our attention on the Lord in our corporate worship time.

If we choose to make our worship experience about performance, we will not produce the necessary environment for Him to inhabit. I am not saying that we should step back from excellence, not in the least. Musicians should play skillfully. Singers should sing with all the expertise in them. When we are before a crowd of people we make the choice whether they see Christ in us or not.

You make the choice as to what kind of environment you live and minister in. Nobody can dictate that. You are the sole controller of your environment either into alignment with the Word of God or not. Make a conscious effort and allow the Holy Spirit to operate through you and this will ensure a Christ like environment.

"Stepping into His presence requires our stepping out of ourselves and into His glory."

Fast Forward:
†
What changes can you make in your environment to make it better?
†
What have you learned about your current environment?

NOTES

CHAPTER THIRTY-THREE
~CONSPIRACY THEORY~

It was signed, sealed and delivered and it was the greatest gift God ever gave to man. No one on earth knew of His plan and yet every person alive would be given the right to have access to it. The price to bring this gift to earth cost heaven its most precious treasure. Nothing was more valuable than the gift God gave man when He gave the world the gift of Jesus Christ. From the moment the news was sounded abroad, in heaven there was an evil plot to circumvent this priceless gift. This evil plot was birthed out of the heart of the worship leader of heaven, Lucifer AKA Satan.

The heart that had once beat only to lead the host of heaven in worship to God the Father had become dark with pride. Satan's desire to worship had somehow become perverted. He wanted the very throne that he knew was soon to be vacant. His pride and greed infected one third of the angels in heaven and incited a ruckus and riot so fierce that God threw Lucifer and his angels out of heaven. From that time until now, Lucifer has been on a crusade to destroy this gift.

Satan does not care whether you are talented or gifted; as a matter of fact that does not impress him one bit because he himself is talented and gifted. He is not concerned about your choir or church board; he doesn't even care that you are a preacher, bishop or an apostle.

What does matter to him is that his covert plan to destroy the power of the gift inside of you and to infiltrate his distorted purpose into your mind, will and emotions succeeds. If he can get his diabolical plan inside your soul and spirit, he will consider his job is done. What he really wants is to simply destroy your faith! If Satan succeeds in destroying our faith, we are powerless, because faith moves God in our behalf.

Satan will talk with you, dance with you, play with you and even shoot baskets with you. He will go to church with you, sing in the choir with you and say amen when the time is right. But! There is one thing he cannot do, and that is the one thing he truly wants more than anything else in this world. He cannot go to heaven with you because he has been eternally banned.

He is hell's secret agent who has found a way to go to choir rehearsal or prayer meetings and remain completely disguised, hidden deep inside of his unassuming victim. Satan loves it when we fail and fall; however, what he cherishes even more is our becoming a vehicle that furthers his agenda. And just how does he accomplish this task? Well my friends, he does it by infiltrating our behavior! If he can get you to proudly convince yourself that you are a James Bond for Christ, he will make your 007 status become 000!

The issue here is that there are forces that are constantly conspiring to keep us out of the position which God has called us to. The enemy will always scheme, connive and launch a full attack in order to throw a wrench into the plan of God. He will conspire with all his agents to keep us from reaching the apex of our calling. The enemy, with everything that is accessible to him, will attempt to circumvent God's call on your life. No matter what he does, he cannot destroy the calling on your life. God has a divine plan and purpose that the enemy cannot destroy.

The enemy uses temptations and distractions to get us off course. However he cannot stop us unless we surrender to him. With everything the enemy brings, and sometimes that is a very formidable force, God has given us the power and victory over him and his tactics. The truth of the matter is the enemy is only successful if we allow ourselves to fall prey to his acts. How many times have I shared with you in the pages of this book that this battle we wage is a mind thing? Our choices make up the final declaration of what will be written about us in the Lamb's Book of Life.

That's why it is so important for us to align ourselves with Philippians 3:14 which states *"I press toward the mark for the prize of the high calling of God in Christ Jesus."* When we 'press,' it means that it takes more than a normal amount of effort to reach a supreme and heavenly goal. This translates into an aggressive act which requires us to run swiftly with all our heart, emotion and passion. What is equally important to understand is that God knows the trials, tribulations, temptations and distractions that we will face along the way.

God knows that within our own strength we cannot be victorious. However, if we purpose in our hearts to be victorious and place our trust and faith in Him through Jesus, His Son, we will no doubt be victorious. God never intended for you to make it alone. If He did, He would have never sent His son Jesus into the world. God never made it impossible for Adam and Eve to reach the forbidden tree, which He could have done, but advised them to keep well clear of it. Satan understands this principle so he also sends you choices and options. The enemy will send us situations and opportunities that would seem so logical, and even legal, just as he did with Adam in the garden.

Have you ever had to make a decision about a potential opportunity, maybe about a potential record deal, a pending tour or even what church you should become a member of? These are all important and practical decisions that we all will make or have made at some point. We must clearly understand that making a bad decision in these practical matters can lead us in the wrong direction which allows a breeding ground for Satan.

"We must understand that anything that the enemy sends will lead us only to the path of eternal death, both spiritually and naturally. Therefore unequivocally our choices and decisions create our future and align us with our destiny."

The peace of God which passes all understanding is a great spiritual gift. We need to use this more diligently for it will guide us into the path of making good sound decisions. As we allow this gift to work in us, we will learn to be in that special place we call the 'zone'.

Zoning requires patience and discipline. You have to be willing to stand by your convictions when zoning. Failure to do so will most certainly place you into a compromising position. You see, what the enemy is trying to do is to get you to sacrifice your future by choosing something that seems necessary in your present condition. In other words, Satan wants to live on credit, which means you are usually satisfying your flesh today at the expense of your soul.

Every conspiracy has a certain element of truth, as I stated earlier. And one example is counterfeit money. A counterfeit dollar has to have some resemblance to the real thing to pass the occasional glance. Greed has its price and since one hundred dollar bills are so abundant these days, the criminals have centered their creative energies on trying to create a passable counterfeit. They spend time and money creating fake money, yet all it takes is one swipe from a specially designed pen across the bill in question to reveal it is counterfeit.

We have been given a similar tool to combat the enemy's efforts to get our life off the path God has intended for us. That tool is the Holy Spirit! That is why it is so important to know God and His ways, for that is the only way you can survive the traps of the enemy. We need to know every nuance and inflection of Him so when the enemy comes and wants to quote counterfeit truth to us, we know how to discern whether it is real.

I often heard the older saints say that if Satan comes and tells you today is Thursday and you know it's Thursday, you should still deem him a liar because he is trying to confuse and distract you. Understand this very simple statement. "Satan uses distractions as a tactic in his conspiracy against us."

As believers, we experience distractions daily, right from the comfort of our homes, on our televisions. We witness distractions right inside our local churches. We experience the distractive designs of the enemy to entice us to do things that we know are clearly contrary to God's plan and call on our life. The enemy has launched a well designed theory that is actually a conspiracy to obtain dominance on your thoughts. One of the most diabolical was the theory that Lucifer proposed to Eve, that God had not actually said not to eat of the Tree of the Knowledge of Good and Evil.

Bringing us into modern times we are all aware of Darwin's Theory of Evolution. Our educational institutions teach as fact something that is by its name a theory. This is how strong the delusion can be when we accept without question his conspiratorial theories. That is why it is so important to cleanse and renew our mind daily.

If the enemy can successfully infiltrate your thought patterns, he does so because your defenses are vulnerable. If your defenses are lowered, the enemy will send a barrage of powerful pleasures and temptations to get you to commit a sin. What he does not tell you is that there are side effects with your making a mental choice to sin. One act of rebellious sin can create shame, guilt, regret, remorse, reproach, ugliness, dirtiness, perversion, confusion, conflict, pain and on and on. He wants you to remain blinded to the pleasures of his conspiracy.

However you were not created to be his servant. You were not created to live under his rule. Every word he speaks is a lie. Every promise he tells you will be broken. Every pinnacle he points you to will be nothing more than a perilous drop off. I want to tell you right here and now that it is time for us to rip his mask off and expose him for the thief of dreams he actually is.

The mask of illusion is easily revealed once we have a clear understanding of what God has said about us and our future. We must make up our minds to be either a successful supernatural being in Christ or a fallen creation under the control of a fallen angel whose destiny is hell. The choice is always ours to make.

Making the right choice unlocks the purpose and plan of God. I want to encourage you to make the right choice!

Fast Forward:
†
What choices or decisions are before you currently?
†
How do you know what is counterfeit?

NOTES

CHAPTER THIRTY-FOUR
~PROVISION FOR VISION~

As I write this book, our world is reeling from one economic crisis to another. The financial failures, stock crashes and unemployment have made an indelible stain on today's society in ways only history will be able to tell. Corporate America has become entrenched with corruption and greed. The overall impact that business and personal failures have made on this fast-changing economic environment has directly affected the faith-based community.

The root cause of our economic situation is poor stewardship. I say this because I have not seen or heard of any alien coming to earth and leaving with a large sum of money. So clearly there is no lack of money. This only points towards bad management which has lead us to this place where millions of people are in financial dismay. Unfortunately, the body of Christ is not exempt from the disastrous trend. Many Christians are now facing repossessions and foreclosures. Some families have to move in with another family in order to make ends meet.

Dual-career families and single-parent households who volunteer their time to much needed community outreaches are vanishing. Special interest groups inside and outside Christianity continue to make demands on discretionary funds and disposable income that dwindle with each passing day.

All these factors are squeezing the fiscal lifeline of the church and have led to many churches' drastically decreasing their faith-based programs, and in some cases they have been completely cut out. Even thriving mega-churches have conceded that they have had to restrict or even reduce their staff in order to meet budget constraints. Many have put potential and exciting plans on the back burner until additional resources are found. This fiscal storm has no regard for theological creed or ideology.

I know many of my friends who are evangelists, musicians and singers have been affected by this backlash. Sounds depressing doesn't it? If all we did was hear the news everyday about what is going wrong, we might get the idea that we will never see better days ahead. The Bible says times will wax worse and worse, BUT! God also says in His Word that he will never leave us or forsake us and that He will supply ALL our needs according to the riches in Christ Jesus! With that declaration of faithfulness from God solidly embedded in my spirit, I can now see where even in this climate there is a greater opportunity for

God to work.

God operates on the principle of order, and any substitution for that principle is a humanistic platform mainly designed for the sake of convenience and immediate pleasure and will always result in confusion and discord.

> *"The character of God gives resources…*
> *Far beyond our human comprehension."*

It is astonishing that every time we stray from God, He finds a way to reprimand us so we can get back on track. This chastisement may come in the form of physical afflictions, emotional distress or even by withholding finances. The fact is God does not operate under the current, past or future economic condition. God is not bankrupt! The truth is that God has His own stimulus package with its own set of rules and spiritual laws. If you want to receive from the stimulus package God has, you must first repent any act that was a transgression of God's law. This is true for an individual. This is true for every single ministry, and it is true for the nations of the world.

Secondly, you must treasure His presence in your life and honor God in the first fruit of your increase. Then finally you must walk in total obedience to His Word. As elementary as this may sound, this is the key to unlocking God's stimulus package. As humans we want security. Knowing what we are going to get and how we are going to get it. However, God does not work like that. Instead of providing us with a thousand dollars then a vision, He first gives us a vision then He requires us to exercise faith for the provision. As we walk in faith and prove God, He makes a provision for the vision.

We should consistently chase the vision of our ministry and call, and then, as we increase and perfect our ministry and vision, God will release the provision. Having no provision should never dictate what you do in your ministry. If it does, you are walking in fear and not trusting God. When there is a lack, it's usually because of our own slothfulness. It's our obedience to the call of God that will cause the resources we so desperately need to gravitate towards us. God is not limited to any one financial source. He is God all-powerful and omniscient. The character of God gives resources far beyond our human comprehension.

There is someone right now holding the very provision necessary for the vision God gave you. That provision may be real estate, equipment, vehicles or straight out cash. Its geographic location may be on the other side of the world or right next door. All God is waiting for is for you to use your faith and be obedient. As you walk in obedience, you will find that money always follows ministry.

Never get it backwards! Ministry does not and should never follow money. This is one of most controversial issues we face in the modern church today. I have seen many in ministry whose personal prosperity goal clouded the plans for God's prosperity in the lives of the very people God assigned them to minister to.

"Where lack is present…
God has already made supernatural provision."

God knows, before you even ask or think, what your needs are. His promise is to supply all your NEEDS according to his riches in glory. We must walk in this promise and do everything righteously possible to allow it to manifest completely in our lives. Remember, God is righteous and anything unrighteous that exists in your life ties God's hands. We need to have a daily cleansing. We must not let sin have dominion over us. Sin is one sure way to cause death to your vision and provision.

May I suggest that you focus on a righteous life style and stay away from the pitfalls of lust which are the base of almost every sin. It seems as if lust has overtaken many of our leadership, causing them to fall and stumble. Lust is very sneaky and puts material things above God. It is not material things or money that is evil. It is the lust for material things and money that supersedes our love of God that is evil. Lust is worshipping or idolizing anything above God.

We will fall into the trap of sin when we transpose our NEEDS into LUST. Lust is the desire to please oneself at the expense of others. This is why it is essential that we stay mindful of excess, which is the prelude to lust. This does not mean we cannot have quality items as Christians. And bear in mind that there is not a God-mandated figure that we need to stay under to avoid experiencing the abundance of God.

Remember in the parable of the talents how God gave the servants different amounts according to their level of faith? When God releases something to you, you will truly know it's from God because there will be no strings attached, no lies will be told to get it and no one gets hurt as a result of it. When the enemy gives something, it is usually birthed out of lust. Anything birthed out of lust will take lust to sustain it. Case in point, if God blesses you with a new car, you are not going to worry about how the payments are being made.

You are not going to worry about how the insurance is going to be paid. On the other hand, if Satan gives you that car, or if it is birthed out of lust, you may find yourself struggling to make the payment which may lead you to do something ungodly to get the money to make the payment. You may even find yourself lying about your residency to obtain cheaper insurance rates. How can we expect God to bless a lie?

From time to time, many of us have fallen victim to some of these practices. The right thing to do is to repent and walk in honesty and trust God to work on your behalf. You may think that you cannot walk away from a life of personal gratification, lust and perversion, but you can. And you will do so if your passion is to serve Him. You can and will if your passion has been ignited and set on the right course.

The moment you are doing what He wants you to do, there will be a wonderful sense of accomplishment that will overcome the feelings you have when you participate in the things of the world. God's kingdom offers everything you need. All you need to do is want Him first and the riches of Heaven will follow. God will always make provision for your vision.

Fast Forward:
†
What steps are you putting in place
to accomplish your vision?
†
How has God provided for your vision?

NOTES

NOTES

CHAPTER THIRTY-FIVE
~THE RIGHT MIND-SET~

"For as he thinketh in his heart, so is he:"
Proverbs 23:7

Everything we seek to do and accomplish begins in the mind. If we want to move our hands, our minds send a signal to our hands and then the movement occurs. Even before we speak, there is a thought that is first registered in our mind. Because of the great importance of our mind, the Bible makes it clear that we should have a renewed mind. A renewed mind is a mind that is God-centered. However, we have to exercise the choice to think either positively or negatively.

God is not going to renew our mind for us. So when adversity comes your way your mindset should be how you are going to resolve it. At all cost do not get consumed by the situation itself. A renewed mind will let you look to the future and allow tomorrow's opportunities to be greater than yesterday's calamities and today's anxieties.

Many of us spend too much time dwelling in the past. Satan will do all he can to get us to focus on everything but what is wrong in our life. If he is successful, he can grab hold of your mind and impact your thinking.

"All Satan wants to do is to get you not to think!"

Satan will do all he can to discourage you. He will even use the very people who are supposed to be a blessing in your life to bring pain and suffering your way. He will cause the very ones who have said how much they love you to turn on you and tear your spirit into pieces. Satan will use those who have anointed you, appointed you and sent you out into the harvest field to slander you and cause you to lose your love for the house of God. All he needs is for them not to have a right mind. So you see, all of us, on both sides of the pulpit, must maintain a renewed and righteous mindset. Just shifting our thinking ever so slightly can allow us the ability to turn our adverse situation into an opportunity. Truly it's an opportunity for us to see God as God the all faithful One.

It's a daily practice for me to renew my mind so I can have the right mind set. If you have been in ministry any length of time, I am quite sure you have been in situations where there was just plain old drama. It may have been precipitated by someone who was territorial, insecure or just rude. These encounters can make your time in ministry quite unfulfilled. When you are in situations like this, you must find common ground. This may require some thought and effort on your part, but the reward will be that you will have a much more productive time in ministry.

"Everyone wants to be loved...
Appreciated, and made to feel important."

I have found that when I choose to change my thought patterns, I can find something positive to draw on. I have used preventive maintenance to calm potential storms. I have used compliments to turn the tide from a negative situation. Try this very successful attitude application. Compliment your adversaries even if there is nothing nice to say about their personality traits. Compliment them about a particular garment they are wearing or better yet, some piece of equipment they are using. Use this method to open a dialogue between you and them. Once communication is established, you have overcome a major hurdle and have taken the first step in bridging the gap. This has worked for me in so many places, so many times.

"Turning adversity into an opportunity...
Is a skill that you must develop."

It's never easy to deal with adverse situations. God's grace will grant you the skill to maneuver through them. You can't run from these situations it's a vital part of ministry. In fact, it is almost certain you will run into someone who will not only challenge you, but will remind about this aspect of ministry.

How you transition through these encounters is important in establishing the right mind set.

THE CREATIVE THOUGHT

A quote from Einstein explains it well: "We can't solve problems by using the same kind of thinking we used when we created them." Problems cannot be solved at the same level they were created. You must expand your thinking to a higher level so you can look down at the problem and then solve it from a higher perspective. We need to be creative and always be thinking about improvements. Try to find a new route to get to your destination. Find new destinations which give you a larger territory. All of this is referred to as forward thinking.

*"Creativity entails breaking out of established patterns...
In order to look at things in a different way."*

Today is the perfect time to renew your mind. Trust me when I tell you that we create our future by what we think and do today. Our thoughts as well as our actions are seeds and they will grow based on what they are fed. Feed your mind with positive thoughts and it with produce the right mind set.

Fast Forward:
†
What thoughts are being fed to your mind?
†
What can you do to change an adverse situation?

NOTES

NOTES

CHAPTER THIRTY-SIX
~DIFFICULT SITUATIONS~

The benediction has just been given and you are leaving service in a positive state only to be confronted by someone telling you about a situation that you truly know nothing about. The one thing you are certain of is that what you are hearing not only grieves your spirit, but presents a very difficult situation that could affect more than one person.

I never enjoy finding myself in the midst of drama and insurmountable situations, but when I do, I choose to allow spiritual discernment to be prevalent. It is then that I realize I have been given the honor of serving God in what I consider to be the most rewarding vocation in the world, despite all the drama.

Where else can you have a job that pays eternal dividends for every life that is changed through the simple act of sharing your testimony? How do you place a value on seeing someone make the choice to accept Christ as his personal savior? How do you place a price on a SOUL?

Understanding that we are truly in the SOUL BUSINESS, we should understand the spirit behind negative, brutal, demanding and angry behavior. Serving God can be fun, exciting, and rewarding; however, there will be moments that bring pain and disappointment. This is not because of God. It's because we serve God among imperfect people who are on different levels of spiritual maturity and have various backgrounds.

The mix of personalities, age ranges and cultures can present many challenges. Navigating through these challenges requires a personal commitment, individual discipline and a life that is centered in the Word of God and prayer. There is no other way around it. God's Word is the neutralizing factor which allows us to see ourselves. Then through the power of the Word we can make the necessary adjustments in difficult situations.

I love it when I see the energy of new Christians entering the Body of Christ. They are filled with such fervor, passion, enthusiasm and excitement and are ready to do whatever it takes to serve God. Without fail, when they are hit with their first confrontation, there is always the possibility that they might lose their joy and excitement. Some are traumatized by people who they looked up to and begin to wonder if what they thought was a spiritual nirvana is perhaps an unrealistic fantasy.

This is not an indictment of any particular person or ministry, but it's a look at the diverse strategies the enemy uses to attack our willingness to serve God. It is also a warning that unless we guard ourselves, we can become too busy with being busy and somehow overlook the people we are trying to reach. It is quite possible that we can become available to being used by the enemy. I am not saying that we can innocently become Satan-possessed. What I am saying is that we must watch out for those little foxes that come in and little by little get us off track.

"It's the smallest things that do the biggest damage in your life."

It doesn't matter what door the enemy uses to come in. Our response should always be based on the direction of the Word of God when moving the enemy out. One way to help battle his strategies is to set up accountable relationships. Remember, iron sharpens iron. It is very important to establish prayer partners and bible study groups. They will keep checks and balances in place so we can stay the course and have ample ammunition for the challenge ahead. There will always be circumstances that come across our path while we are minding our own business, serving God and then get suddenly blindsided with an altercation. These conflicts may even be among fellow believers.

If Jesus, being the son of God, had difficulty with his disciples, why would we think that we would be exempt from discord among the brethren today? To have a team of creative individuals operating without difficulties is a major accomplishment. It takes wisdom, maturity, and stability to serve among individual personalities in a team setting. However, with the "Fruit of the Spirit" in operation, you should be successful in obtaining a positive outcome.

Team members have to collectively accept that they are cooperatively involved with something bigger than themselves that one member does not make the team but the team makes each member stronger. Team members have to be willing to die to their own fleshly desires and let go of their personal agendas. Having dress codes serves a deeper function than visual uniformity; it promotes oneness among the team.

Our own personal and secret agendas help only to magnify difficult situations in ministry. We have to be able and willing to put aside personal feelings. We must learn how to live out the same prayer Christ prayed in the Garden of Gethsemane just days before he was to face crucifixion; "Father, not my will but thine be done." What's the use in fighting to be correct while in the process you are doing harm? Many times in the heat of conflicts we say things that we don't mean and they spark an environment which makes the ground fertile for Satan to plant discord and division.

Some of these difficult situations in which we find ourselves are our own doing. These situations will always be encountered, even while doing the right thing. Personal success or failure is usually guided by our response to any given situation. What is important here is that God is using these situations to build character in you. It takes trials and tribulations to bring forth the substance and character that God wants you to have. I want to encourage you to continue to walk in the spirit so you will not fall prey to difficult situations.

Fast Forward:

†

What are you doing to avoid conflict and promote a drama free environment for service?

†

What causes people in service to God to act in a rude, aggressive manner?

NOTES

CHAPTER THIRTY-SEVEN
~FRUSTRATION~

When we accept the call of God on our lives, a passion and desire begins to burn deep inside which motivates us to want to accomplish something special for the kingdom of God. This passion and desire may be expressed in one of many ways. For instance, a singer may experience a deep hunger and desire to share their gift with the world. Some may go the route of pursuing a recording career while others may prefer to share their gift by singing in the church choir. No matter which path you choose, you will undoubtedly feel a deep compulsion that gives you the drive necessary to do what it takes to become a success.

While on the path to fulfilling this need to succeed, there may be times when out of the blue you are hit with an obstacle which turns everything upside down. What began as a passionate drive to succeed has just hit its first wall or, better yet, its first real "challenge". Challenges are a major part of every successful campaign and all too often seem insurmountable, which in turn produces frustration.

I have discovered throughout the years of ministering at churches all over the world that a level of unspoken frustration exists in the creative arts departments. Whether it is derived from lateral relationships among the group members or issues dealing with leadership, the frustration is apparent. This is nothing new when you think about it. Satan and his angels created chaos and war in the heavens all because they became frustrated that they were not given the same position as God. That same attitude which permeated Satan's crew has found its way into society today and is most often making its presence known in the church.

Battles between pastors and music directors are on the top of the frustration list, but let's not just stop there. There are other battles that occur between elders, departmental heads, choir members and members in general, but nothing rips apart the corporate body any more than when the worship in the house has been thrown into chaos.

"Where there is chaos, there will be a constant presence of frustration and anger."

There are several reasons why frustration can be found in the heart of those serving in the houses of worship. One reason is when our expectations are not met. To overcome this emotional trap we must learn how to guard our hearts.

> *"Above all else, guard your heart,*
> *for it is the wellspring of life."*
> **Proverbs 4:23**

Guarding our heart means managing our expectations. Many times our expectations are unrealistic. I remember a situation that happened at a church not too long ago. One of the church employees had a laptop computer he brought home at night and back to work the next day. He knew all the other employees fairly well and had what would be considered solid relationships with them. They all enjoyed a strong Christian bond among them so it was nothing to leave personal items unsupervised.

One day the laptop came up missing and its owner became very angry and frustrated. His first thought was how could this happen in the house of God, which was where he made his first mistake. His expectation was that everyone in that environment was honest and upstanding. He experienced a rude awakening when he realized it was necessary to properly secure one's personal valuables, even in God's house. It's important to manage your expectations and not take things for granted, as this will minimize the chance of disappointment and frustration occurring.

Lack of communication is another major cause of frustration in our houses of worship. People in general function better when they have knowledge of what they are supposed to do and when it is to get done. A clear outline of the requirements will establish a barometer for the organization. For a successful worship experience there needs to be solid communication between the senior pastor and the worship leader. When these two leaders are not in sync, you can be sure there will be chaos.

This same principle applies to the band, choir, departmental heads, elders and members. If there is not a clearly defined communication system in place, there is the potential for chaos.

Frustration leads to chaos when there are conflicting points of view that arise due to the lack of a plan designed to establish harmony. Division is the key component which allows chaos to fester in our houses of worship. There is no doubt that it takes prayer to reverse the effects of chaos and division, but it also takes a concerted physical effort to redirect its negative impact. You must be proactive in order to effect a change. We must never forget that we are imperfect people serving a perfect God. It is never God's intention to mislead or deceive us; therefore, when we find ourselves frustrated with a situation, we must remember it is not God's doing.

"You can sense frustration when you are presented with unpredictable situations."

Let me offer an example of an unpredictable situation. I have experienced worship services where the pastor made changes that were not communicated earlier. For example, he asked for a song that was not recently rehearsed. This has the potential of sending a jolt of frustration through the musicians and singers, right smack in the middle of worship. How the musicians and singers handle this new directive reveals a great deal about the unity between them and the pastor. If they are flexible and understand the moving of the Holy Spirit, everyone is benefited by it.

We must know how to handle the unknown and unseen opportunities that arise unexpectedly. We must be able to handle efficiently the unthinkable events that seem to pop up from time to time. It is important to walk in the Spirit and use discernment when we are faced with any one of these scenarios.

In the end this discernment will enable us to steer clear of hitting a wall of frustration while serving the Lord in His house. If you feel like you are facing insurmountable frustration let me to encourage you to dig down deep in your spirit and pull from your spirit man. From the depth of your spirit you can do something that will make a positive change.

As we grow in our calling and experience, we will come to realize that things are not as bad as they initially appear. Many times things seem much worse simply because we are caught up in the middle of the chaos and cannot see the big picture. Taking a break and reflecting on our core values and the purpose of our calling will help us to keep things in perspective.

I can assure you that if you stay positive, any season of frustration will pass. A positive mind is far more open to solutions and answers than a negative one that thinks it's just "hopeless" and responds with the attitude "what's the use?" A closed mind will not be able to see the possible solutions when they do come along.

Remain positive and make positive changes. One way to do this is to eliminate the "noise" and simplify the environment. When trying to solve a problem, use caution that you do not get so wrapped up in trying to find the solution that you add unnecessary clutter and noise. Once the clutter is removed and the noise is gone, you then have simplified the need to take action by exercising your faith.

Let me offer another example. If an offense has occurred between you and someone else and it is causing you to be frustrated, do something about it. Remember you always have options and unlimited avenues that will lead to a solution. You just need to get quiet and brainstorm and figure them out. Tell yourself you need to come up with three possible options to what you're dealing with. Just knowing that you have lots of options will help to make you feel better. You won't feel like you are trapped in a boxed canyon of negativity. From your list, figure out the best direction and do not hesitate to take action. Believe in faith that you will have a positive outcome.

Many of us like to travel the path of least resistance. We will do anything to avoid having to deal with a negative situation and will do almost anything possible to create a far more positive result. It's important to keep taking steps forward in an effort to make a positive change. Prayerfully ask the Holy Spirit to guide your steps and more importantly to put a guard on your tongue. If you use this application you will make it past any temporary bump in the road. As Thomas Edison said, "Many of life's failures are people who did not realize how close they were to success when they gave up" and "Surprises and reverses can serve as an incentive for great accomplishment."

In summation, if you want a long term solution to a frustrating situation, focus on the changes you want to see happen. Go back and revisit that moment you felt the Holy Spirit drawing you toward your surrender to your calling and reaffirm your relationship with Christ. Make a confession as to what you want the desired outcome to be.

> *"It's our confession that establishes*
> *The atmosphere for our procession."*

Too many times we get so wrapped up trying to solve one problem that we forget what we were originally trying to accomplish. Try not to ask yourself, "Why did this happen?" Asking questions like that will keep you rooted in the past. While there is a lot to learn from the past, we should limit our past experiences to their educational value. If they don't offer a present day solution to a current problem, they should not hold a major position in our mind, much less take advantage of our time.

If you truly want to eliminate frustration, you have to be willing to overlook past, present and future obstacles. They will serve only as a distraction from your reaching the depth of your creative call. As you add depth to your relationship with God and those around you in the Body of Christ, you will experience less frustration.

Fast Forward:
†
Are you experiencing frustration at your house of worship?
†
What steps have you put in place to eliminate frustration?

NOTES

CHAPTER THIRTY-EIGHT
~WHO ARE YOU REALLY~

You just concluded your final performance of the night, the curtain has closed and it's just you and God. Physically you are exhausted from the excitement of the evening. Spiritually you are on a cloud because you have the assurance that God has met you in your creative moments. Now as you exit this venue and arrive into the solitude of your private place, who is there to meet you? Which you is really you? Was the experience as an actor simply a role or was it an extension of you the worshipper?

It's easy to hide behind our talent because for most that is our public identity. However the real you does not reside in your talent but in the substance of choices and decisions that govern your life, demonstrated in your character. It's your character that is the true representation of who you really are.

*Our talent and artistry may identify us,
but it is our character that defines us.*

A question I would like to pose to you for you to think about is this, "What are the solutions in overcoming the decline of character and integrity in ministry today?" I am going to be generic in my brief descriptions because I might hit too close to home with some of the illustrations I will use to back them up. So, before we continue, let me first state that I am not sitting in judgment with my comments here.

I, myself, am thankful to God for His redemptive process which has restored me when I was walking in disobedience. What I am bringing light to is the fact that we have situations that have arisen in the body of Christ that do not reflect the character of Christ and His Kingdom. Anyone of us at anytime can be led astray; that's why it is so important to keep one another lifted in prayer. I have identified a few steps that, if followed, will certainly help to keep you on the straight and narrow. Okay, let's get started!

First, if in doubt, don't! When you are in doubt about a decision or a proposed proceeding, allow more time to think and pray it through. Then seek sound godly counsel from those you know, who have your spiritual best interest at heart. Another way to avoid an integrity failure is to avoid all appearance of evil.

*"Shun, do not associate;
abstain from any appearance of evil"*
1 Thessalonians 5:22

Don't allow yourself to get into questionable situations with someone of the opposite sex or with a person of the same sex. Have accountability relationships. Remember this simple truth, there is a reason why the disciples went out by twos in the early church. There should never be a situation where you are alone in an intimate setting with someone of the opposite sex other than your spouse. Without a witness present, you are simply inviting trouble by playing with potential fire. Sadly, we tend to look at the sexual issues to be the 'end-all be-all' when it comes to issues of integrity, while there are many more issues that warrant our attention.

The integrity of your words are just as important! Our elders held to an old statement that "your word is your bond," meaning that you follow through on the things you commit to. Are you honest in your communication and clearly express your intentions without any room for erroneous interpretation? Your word should be as trustworthy and binding as your signature or your swearing under oath in a court of law to tell the truth.

Another reason that our Christian artists and ministers have lost their integrity is because of the ambitions which are born out of the flesh. There is nothing wrong with our striving to be the best we can be and reach our highest potential, which is one of the major themes of this book. However, we must be careful of what and who are driving the motivation. The Bible says that whatever we do, we should do it heartily and that our focus should be on pleasing the Lord, not on receiving the accolades of what the world views as success.

*"Whatever you do, do your work heartily,
as for the Lord rather than for men."*
Colossians 3:23

We should certainly give our best, but that does not necessarily mean that we will be the best. "Having to be the best" artist or minister will certainly place the focus on attaining success by the world's standards. I must caution you that this opens the door for you to make poor decisions. These poor decisions usually take you down the road to becoming a compiler of material things. Then, when you have reached the height of the world's concept of success, you will feel spiritually invincible and let your guard down, and that is when moral failure often takes root.

We all are human and are prone to error. When we do fall short, do we face up to it or do we try to cover it up or try to place the blame on someone else? When Jonah was running away from God and the will of God, he took the blame for the chaos caused by his disobedience which affected harmfully everyone around him. What an admirable decision! But if you look at what he had to go through to get to that point, you might see that he had what we call an epiphany, especially being cooped up in the belly of a whale for days!

> *"He said to them, 'I am a Hebrew, and I fear the LORD GOD of heaven who made the sea and the dry land.' Then the men became extremely frightened and they said to him, 'How could you do this?' For the men knew that he was fleeing from the presence of the LORD, because he had told them, so they said to him, 'What should we do to you that the sea may become calm for us?' for the sea was becoming increasingly stormy. He said to them, "Pick me up and throw me into the sea. Then the sea will become calm for you, for I know that on account of me this great storm has come upon you."* Jonah 1:9-12

At all cost avoid making mistakes! When you make a mistake, immediately confess your sin and address the issue with those who may have been affected by it.

> *"If we confess our sins,*
> *He is faithful and righteous to forgive us our sins*
> *and to cleanse us from all unrighteousness."*
> **1 John: 1:9**

About your decisions and challenges, answer honest questions of those with whom you are in covenant relationship and nobody else. Be humble in spirit and heart and willing to accept correction and discipline. Maintaining a life of sound character and integrity is a lifelong process. Spend private time with the Lord every day; be up front with yourself and those who you are serving under about your weakness and challenges. Live a life where you get all the facts before making crucial decisions, and don't allow yourself to be put in compromising situations.

You will find a great deal of peace and contentment if you are able to identify with the Apostle Paul and joyfully say, "I am not ashamed: for I know whom I have believed, and am persuaded that He is able to keep that which I have committed unto him against that day." It's one thing to feel you have integrity in the eyes of your fellow man, but the true worth of integrity is not how man sees you but how God sees you.

ACTIVATION:

Activation means putting the pedal to the metal and taking action. Taking command of a situation and bringing it under control requires understanding the power of authority. There are singers who can sing nicely and then there are singers who take command of a song. They make it their own as a master towards a slave. You have to move forward with boldness because the enemy of your soul will try to eliminate everything that you throw at him. We have the power over him and cannot be defeated as long as we stand on the Word of God. Even if we come up short in a battle, the Bible tells us that we can know that in the end we will win. Satan knows this too, so he sends things your way to discourage you so that you don't even put up a fight.

EXECUTION:

Executing is fundamentally the capability to make change and "MAKE IT HAPPEN." You have to be driven and determined to make things happen. People who make things happen do not look at obstacles as excuses but as stepping stones to finding new solutions. They are relentless and work tirelessly to accomplish a task and reach their goals. Their strength lies in the ability to catch a vision and make it a reality.

So, to wrap up this chapter let me make this observation. If you are facing a challenge in a relationship, whether at church or in your personal life, and there seems to be some level of conflict, could it be that there is something wrong on your side of the fence? When we prefer to point out the splinter in someone's eye while ignoring the beam in our own, we are in a sad state.

If all you do is find fault while never addressing your own shortcomings, you will experience the same chastisement and discipline that Jonah did. God may not let a whale swallow you up, but you might have a whale of a problem arise from a sea of trouble. The choice to change is always yours. If there is one golden thread that runs through this book, it is that we must embrace the new creation God has created us to be. It is our decisions and choices which will eventually advertise to the world who we are and what our agenda in life is.

Throughout the pages of this book I have shared many experiences from my personal life and ministry, not so that you will think highly of me but to offer my shortcomings so you learn from them and not repeat them. If I can save you from making similar mistakes and errors so that the kingdom of Heaven will be exalted in the earth, then to God Be The Glory!

Now, ask yourself how you feel about your decisions and experiences and see if you can find areas where you can improve or even eradicate from your personality. Toxic personality traits are highly radioactive and can spread the infection of error faster than you can blink your eye. Bad news, along with bad people and bad experiences, always gets the front page headline. Take my advice and go for the Good News!

Fast Forward:

†

What are you currently doing to protect your character and integrity?

†

What personal challenges are affecting your character and integrity?

NOTES

CHAPTER THIRTY-NINE
~SERVICE~

The word 'service' has long been the core value when providing quality business to consumers. Most large corporations that offer products to the public have a customer service department. They know how important it is to provide solutions to any complaint or faulty product. Service is actually one of the foundation stones of ministry. Service begins when we are first obedient to God and to those in leadership over us. Now that we have established service to be part of the foundation of ministry, let's look at some of the application levels.

Service should always be based on the Word of God and how it can bring growth and positive change into people's lives. Those who serve with their talent and creative abilities enhance the worship experience and artistically amplify the message of the Gospel of Jesus Christ. The creative arts ministry serves as a support system for those who are actively engaged in serving others.

"When you are gifted in the area of music, dance or drama you will always gravitate to a ministry where your gifts are in-sync with the creative dynamics of that body."

The body of Christ in this new millennium is blessed to have service ministries which operate on the highest levels of professionalism and excellence through multi-media and creative arts presentations and can rival most secular productions. These service ministries operate under a corporate mandate to present the gospel in a manner that will attract a demographic that normally would not respond to a traditional church setting. Although contemporary in their approach, the multi-media ministries serve as a vital part of today's evangelism outreach.

Another way today's church provides its congregation service is through various ministries in the church, such as the benefit of providing a spiritual covering. This covering is a blessing to both the member and the local church when it is established and supported by way of accountability.

This accountability requires one to wholly embrace and accept spiritual authority. The discipline required to maintain accountability is simply doing the things you have to do and need to do consistently, even when you don't feel like making the effort. Without exception accountability is a necessary component for every aspect of service.

> *"Growth Can Be Painful At Times…*
> *Pain Is Necessary For Maturity and Growth."*

It is essential that you find a place where you can serve God and His people. Once you have located the local assembly you believe God has called you to serve in, it's time to get busy. Never allow yourself to become spiritually inactive. Remember, service is not about you, it's about sharing the Gospel of Jesus Christ by virtue of engaging your natural and spiritual gifts. Service in ministry emphasizes the development of character.

Your skills, talents and abilities may take you to high levels of greatness, but you will only be able to sustain those levels by the depth of your character. Good character will enable you to uphold a high standard of integrity while being able to discern right from wrong and possess good judgment versus bad judgment. Your character will constantly be tested in the growth process; therefore, humility is a vital step in character development.

> *"When You Have Found The Place*
> *Where You Believe God Has Sent You….*
> *Be Teachable."*

Let me go back to where I left off telling you about how I joined a church in the first place. Once I had made my decision to join a church, I found out that they had a rule that I had to be a member for one year and attend several classes before I could participate in the music department. The truth is I was appalled at the demand they made that I go through all that time and effort! I thought, they don't know all that I have to offer or what I have done.

I did not know it then but this was exactly what God wanted for me. God knew I was talented because He gave me the gift. What I was to learn was that all of this was exactly what He planned for me so I could understand the importance of service. So reluctantly I went through the process, which was required, by the church to participate in the music department.

After the year passed I began to get concerned because the ministry had not contacted me to participate. The natural man inside me said "Why don't you just leave? You can find many other ministries who would love to have you." The spirit man said, "Wait, for God is working on your behalf and God knows the time and He is totally in control."

Well, to condense the story, I ended up waiting another year. That additional time was needed because there were still things in my character that required additional work. I can happily say that today my service to Him benefited from that process and now I understand why the extended wait period was necessary. I had to humble myself and work in full compliance with God's plan. You see, prior to this happening, my concern was all about my reputation and not my character. There were many things in my life and character that needed to be worked on and developed so I could go to the next level of service, spiritually and professionally.

It seemed like that year flew by at the speed of light. I actually began to enjoy and appreciate serving God on a new level which was not based on my musical talent but on my love for Him. Please take note that it's not about what you do but how you do it, when you do it, and who you do it for.

True service is birthed out of the willingness to die to self and allow God to live through you.

Fast Forward:
†
Have you found a place where you can serve God and His people?
†
What is it in your character that still needs attention?

NOTES

CHAPTER FORTY
~PRACTICAL APPLICATION~

Remember that passion is the gasoline that fuels our calling. Now that we have gas in the car, we all know it's not practical or intelligent to drive recklessly down any given street. The result of doing that would produce harmful and dangerous circumstances. So when all is said and done, we need to make wise and practical decisions when it comes to our calling.

For the past thirty years I have been connected to the music industry in one way or another. Having many close connections in that industry has given me a position to watch the trends and the new order of doing business. Back in the 1980's the method of operation was to do all you could as an artist to get discovered and ultimately to get that lucrative recording contract. That was the goal and the mind set of just about every artist. I was very fortunate to work with many prominent people in the industry and had my share of contract offers. However, as the nineties began to wind down and after the events of September 11, 2001, the music industry dramatically changed.

In 1998, I remember signing a distribution deal with *Diamante Music Distribution* and this deal was really a great situation for me because it enabled me to get my music into the market place without all of the limitations that come with signing a record deal.

Shortly after the September 11, 2001 events, I was informed that *Diamante Music Distribution* would no longer distribute my products. I was really devastated by this news. However, through this entire disheartening situation I learned some very practical lessons. The first thing I learned was that my calling and talent had nothing to do with a record or distribution deal. God never called me to that.

Yes, these situations were vitally important in getting my message and music into the public arena, but it was not the main course God had laid out for me. Many artists, including myself, were under the misguided notion that you need some kind of record deal to be validated as an artist.

"God never calls us to be caught up in our passion…
Even though passion fuels our calling."

If you get distracted by the passion of the call, you will miss the essence of the call itself. The Bible is very clear when it states that we are to go out and take the gospel to the uttermost parts of the world. It never placed a premium on the vehicle or medium we use to take the gospel around the world.

It's like looking at an airplane as the destination. Though the plane is important to get you there, it's not the destination.

Another lesson I learned was that when God calls you to do anything, He gives you the ability, wisdom and the gifts to accomplish it. I want you to look at the word 'gift' from another angle. See the word from this viewpoint, that you have been entrusted or given the wherewithal to accomplish a certain task. It's already there inside of you, much like a treasure chest with a lock on it. All you have to do is to unlock it. You already have the talent inside you which is the key. All you need to do is to discover the passion necessary to use the key and then open the lock and release the gift.

While I was running after distribution and record deals, God had already given me the blue print to get the job done. I was just looking in the wrong place. Sometimes knowing which treasure chest to open can mean either an immediate promotion or a season of preparation. You cannot know what is inside an opportunity, but you can rest assured of the treasure inside of yourself.

There was a period of seven years when I did not release any new music. Did this mean that I was not making full use of the gifts God had instilled in me? Not releasing any new music to the public had nothing to do with my call. As a matter of fact, I did more ministry-related events all over the world during that period.

One of the reasons I believe I was able to do this was because I did not have the pressure to sell product or to meet contractual obligations of a record or distribution deal. I was actually free to do what God called me to do. But, even in this period of commercial silence, I believed that it was still important for me to have a commercially released product.

Don't get me wrong, I understood that the product was not the purpose, it was the vehicle. Coming to this understanding enabled me to walk away from many opportunities and situations that presented themselves to me that would have taken time away from the purpose of my calling. In the same manner, there are those situations that God will use to complete the plan He designed for us. One such situation must be shared before we part.

In 2008 I was informed of a very interesting conference that would take place in Cannes, France. It was called the Midem Conference. It was considered to be the world's premier destination for music connections and industry knowledge sharing. I had heard of this conference for many years and decided to go. I made some very interesting contacts and came home with a greater insight into the world's view of the music industry. A few weeks later I received a phone call from a contact I had given my card to, offering me a world-wide distribution deal. I accepted it and still enjoy the relationship to this day.

But that is not the entire story. As the distribution contracts were being finalized, I suddenly remembered a word that had come from the Lord in 2007 concerning the favor and promotion that was to come my way. It had taken one year before that word came to pass, but God was faithful to His word and here I was living it. My global distribution deal was a reality.

It took my getting into a different vehicle in a different country for that word to come to pass, but it happened just as God said it would. Waiting on the answer may not be pleasant, but when the answer comes there is nothing like it.

After all these years and after learning all these lessons, here I am writing this book with that same passion for Christ I have had for music and ministry. This is a different vehicle that I have come to accept as part of the gifts God has given to me to use for His glory. To you who have read these pages, I pray that you have gained some new knowledge and have experienced a change in your life. I hope that you are now able to see clearer the plan of God for your life and the need for His divine guidance in everything you do and say naturally, spiritually and creatively.

Being an award winning artist has its rewards. Being a servant of the Most High God has even greater rewards. The music industry is today a totally different kind of business from when I first entered it. The days of waiting for the record store to get the new albums in on the shelf are over. The internet now delivers music to the world almost as fast as it is being produced. Literally hundreds of thousands of musicians now fill the air with their music. And right in the middle of all of this wonderful music are the psalmists who lift up the name of Christ and exalt the Father in heaven.

Technology provides us with a delivery system that now helps us to do the work of the Lord faster and more efficiently. Right now, if you have never heard one note of my musical work, you can go on the internet to *www.melholder.com* and experience for yourself the artistry of the gift God has given me.

No matter where you are in the world right now as long as you can connect to the internet you can be connected to so many things. You can shop online and never leave your home. You can communicate with people all around the world and never step outside of your house. But! God did not create us for technology, He created us for fellowship. Therefore we should not allow technology to be our end of all ends. We must use it as a valued vehicle only. There is still nothing more exciting than to be sitting in a live setting hearing music.

Likewise there is a great benefit to worshiping in your home with my music or some other artist's music. But there is nothing more vital than being in the company of like-minded believers as you corporately worship God. What I am trying my best to say to you here is that all of what we have at our disposal must be used with wisdom and practicality. Anything done in extreme, even if it is a good thing, is error. Everything we come into contact with can be used for either good or evil. We make the choice!

You are about to read what I call My Pledge. It is a very important part of your reading experience in this book. But I want to ask you one last thing before you turn the page.

Will you take a moment and lift your face heavenward and give God thanks for all that He has done for you, through you and in you? Will you praise Him for the gifts and talents He has placed inside of you? Will you thank Him for opening heaven up and blessing you with all that He has blessed you with?

Will you promise Him that you will not fail to nurture the talent you have and to mature in your ministry to Him and for Him? Then, when you have taken the time to truly show Him your heart is full of gratitude and thankfulness, read on and join me in My Pledge.

Fast Forward
†
Is there something that you desire which will greatly enhance your ministry?
†
What are you doing to obtain this desire?

NOTES

CHAPTER FORTY-ONE
~MY PLEDGE~

We have come to the last chapter of *The Pursuit of Your Creative Call,* and there is yet one very important step for you to make, and this one is more important than all the previous steps you have made while reading this book.

Before you make this final step, let me make it very clear to you that this step can and will establish you as a servant of God, one who is ready to give their life and talents for the advancement of the Kingdom of Heaven.

Please read the pledge out loud and when you arrive at the end, would you spend time worshiping God and giving Him all the praise and glory for granting you not only eternal life but also the wonderful gifts and talents? Now take this final step and join me, along with thousands of other creative artists all over the world who live to be an expression of God in the earth. Say these words aloud, please.

My Pledge

I acknowledge the importance of the CALL
GOD has placed on my life.

I understand the importance of the GIFT
GOD has given me stewardship over.

I purpose in my heart to GIVE
My total commitment to GOD.

I realize that GOD has placed tremendous VALUE
On what HE has called me to accomplish.

I will strive to bring GOD GLORY

By faithfully administering
the creative abilities entrusted to me.

I honor the TALENTS
HE has entrusted to me

I honor the ABILITIES
HE has entrusted to me

I honor the Skills
HE has entrusted to me.

I understand GOD requires
my MOST PRIZED POSSESSION,

**My TIME, ENERGY and DEDICATION!
I will diligently seek GOD
For SPIRITUAL DIRECTION for my GIFTS.**

**I will consistently PRAY for PROTECTION
Over my LIFE and GIFTS.**

I will embrace GOD'S PLAN for my LIFE!

**I will do all that is within my POWER
Through the direction and power of the HOLY SPIRIT
To use my GIFTS to win SOULS!**

**Everything I do will be to ADVANCE
THE KINGDOM OF GOD
here on Earth.**

AMEN!

If you have made this pledge along with me, I would deeply appreciate hearing from you. I trust the journey we have been on through these pages has been an insightful and inspiring one.

Until we meet face to face here on this earth or in the presence of the Lord of Glory in Heaven, God Richly Bless You!

Creatively Living In Him

Mel Holder

NOTES

ABOUT MEL HOLDER

Minister, Musician, Producer, Arranger, Composer, Performer, Ambassador and Promoter of the healing power of Jesus Christ, Mel's unique gifting has touched numerous lives worldwide. From the ancient Asian city of Okinawa, Japan through the secular Muslim nation of Azerbaijan to the remote communities of post apartheid, South Africa, throughout the Caribbean, Europe and the socialist country of Cuba and the USA, this anointed Psalmist can be heard performing the melody of his message; The healing of the Nations and Preparation for the Return of Christ.

Born in Brooklyn NY, of Panamanian decent, Mel was a testimony in the making. From the age of six years old, Mel was hindered from being able to fully participate in all of life's youthful activities due to asthma. However, God taught him, through that challenge, to become a focused relentless warrior. This physical impairment made it quite difficult for Mel to breathe normally but at the age of nine he picked up his sister's clarinet out of curiosity and began to make haunting sounds with it.

Mel's family immediately knew that this was Divine intervention since such an act was deemed impossible based on his physical condition. This was a testament to the undeniable power of God's healing touch and the beginning of miracles in Mel's journey to musical manhood.

Barbara Streisand, Shaggy, James D-Train Williams and Pastor James Cymbala are all part of the Alumni of Erasmus Hall Institute of Performing Arts in Brooklyn NY, where Mel excelled among his musical peers. On numerous occasions he received write-ups in the local newspapers as to his exceptional musicianship.

During Mel's growing popularity on the fast track the Lord decided that his preliminary training was completed and that it was time for Mel to be sanctified for His work only. He was enjoying great financial success, attending Miami Dade college by day, and performing on Miami Beach by night when he was forced to leave everything that he had work for all his life and return to his mother's home in Brooklyn, New York, where the climate was more conducive to his health condition. Mel's trip back home to New York placed him at his appointed hour with destiny to receive Jesus in his life as personal Lord and Savior.

This life defining moment happened under the ministry of the late Nellie Leakey in Brooklyn NY. Pastor Leakey, and her son Ronnie Leakey Jr., became Mel's early pastor and mentor in the gospel. While at one of the church youth retreats in the Pocono Mountains in Pennsylvania, Mel met a very young and exuberant preacher, B. Courtney McBath, who was the guest speaker on this trip. Minister McBath baptized Mel, and began a life long mentorship with him.

Mel enrolled at United Christian College where he studied evangelism. He would later be introduced to the ministry of then Christian Life Center (currently known as Christian Cultural Center). Now under the teaching and ministry of Dr. A.R. Bernard, Mel Holder has gathered spiritual principles and roots which powered him into music ministry.

Mel's first CD was released in 1997 and since then Mel has maintained a very aggressive ministry schedule which presents opportunities for him to minister to a wide range of event; nationally and internationally.

Although Mel's role in Christian music is still being defined as an innovative Psalmist, he stands firmly on the healing that he has received from God. Mel can sustain long notes which are humanly impossible which serves to remind himself of the wonderful miracle working power of God he experienced as a young man. Today, Mel continues to present the message of New Life in Christ though his music, message and positive ministry.

This is Mel's first book. If you have enjoyed reading **The Pursuit of Your Creative Call**, you will certainly enjoy his music ministry also. He is available for interviews, conferences, and worship engagements.

Availability:
Worldwide by arrangement

Contact:
Psalmist Music Group
P.O. Box 340533
Rochdale Village, NY 11434
(718) 485-5550
Email: Mel@MelHolder.com

PRODUCTS

Coming Soon!
Music Book Vol. 2
Back To Basic

CD's $15.97
Order at
www.melholder.com

Music Book Vol. 1

Or send your check or
money order to:

Now & Forever
(The Continuation)

Psalmist Music Group
P.O. Box 340533
Rochdale Village,
New York 11434

718-485-5550

A Gift So Special

Now & Forever